Marrakech, High Atlas & Essaouira

Julius Honnor

Credits

Footprint credits
Editor: Felicity Laughton
Production and layout: Emma Bryers
Maps: Kevin Feeney

Managing Director: Andy Riddle
Content Director: Patrick Dawson
Publisher: Alan Murphy
Publishing Managers: Felicity Laughton,
Jo Williams, Nicola Gibbs
Marketing and Partnerships Director:
Liz Harper
Marketing Executive: Liz Eyles
Trade Product Manager: Diane McEntee
Account Managers: Paul Bew, Tania Ross
Advertising: Renu Sibal, Elizabeth Taylor
Trade Product Co-ordinator: Kirsty Holmes

Photography credits
Front and back cover: Dreamstime

Printed in Great Britain by CPI Antony Rowe,
Chippenham, Wiltshire

Publishing information
Footprint Focus Marrakech, High Atlas &
Essaouira
1st edition
© Footprint Handbooks Ltd
June 2012

ISBN: 978 1 908206 71 8
CIP DATA: A catalogue record for this book
is available from the British Library

® Footprint Handbooks and the Footprint
mark are a registered trademark of
Footprint Handbooks Ltd

Published by Footprint
6 Riverside Court
Lower Bristol Road
Bath BA2 3DZ, UK
T +44 (0)1225 469141
F +44 (0)1225 469461
footprinttravelguides.com

Distributed in the USA by Globe Pequot
Press, Guilford, Connecticut

The content of Footprint Focus Marrakech,
High Atlas & Essaouira has been taken
directly from Footprint's Morocco Handbook
which was researched and written by
Julius Honnor.

Contents

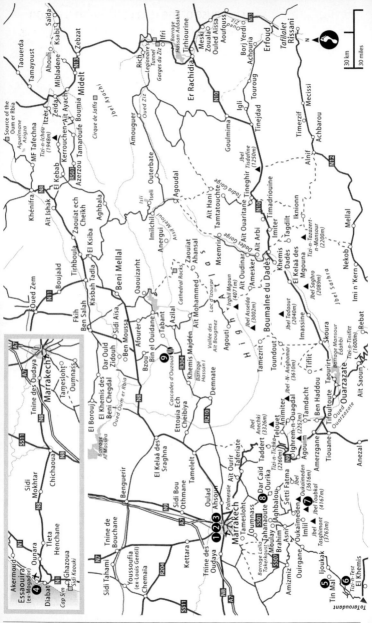

The Red City, so called because of the terracotta wash used on its buildings, lies within reach of both the cool High Atlas valleys and, beyond arid plains to the west, the coast. Focus points are the elegant 12th-century Koutoubia Mosque and the Jemaâ el Fna 'square', famed for its seething mass of entertainments and open-air restaurants. Around them stretches the medina, a place of narrow streets, flat-roofed houses and minarets. The souks are thronged with handicrafts of every shape and size, from silken caftans and pottery drums to carved wooden chests and the orange-woollen expanses of Chichaoua carpets.

West of Marrakech, the photogenic fishing port of Essaouira has been an important port for centuries and its high walls have been battered by various sea powers, as well as Atlantic waves. Its fishing industry survives, though the focus is increasingly on tourism, and the surrounding beaches are popular with windsurfers.

Snow-topped for half the year, the High Atlas rise out of the plains south of Marrakech. West to east they stretch across Morocco from the Atlantic coast just north of Agadir until they fade into the desert on the Algerian border. In winter, there is scope for skiing; in spring, apple and cherry blossom fills the valleys with colour, and, in summer, the cooler air is a draw for escapees from the oppressive cities. All year round there are good walking opportunities, from short strolls to serious treks.

Within easy day-trip distance of Marrakech, the Toubkal National Park, named for Jbel Toubkal, the highest peak in North Africa, has long been a draw for tourists. Other popular destinations, include the pretty Setti Fatma in the Ourika Valley and the ski resort of Oukaïmeden. The striking, restored mosque of Tin Mal is high on the spectacular road to the Tizi-n-Test pass. Heading south Is another dramatic pass, the Tizi-n-Tichka, and the village of Telouet, with its brooding Glaoui fortress. Further east are the Cascades d'Ouzoud, Morocco's highest waterfalls, and the beautiful high valley of the Aït Bougmez.

Planning your trip

Best time to visit Marrakech, High Atlas and Essaouira

Marrakech is a good destination all year round, although the heat can be oppressive during the day from July to late September. Summer and autumn are good for walking and climbing in the High Atlas; spring can be too, though lingering snow often makes higher routes difficult unless you have good equipment. The Jbel Saghro, south of the High Atlas, is a winter walking destination, as are the Anti-Atlas. Windsurfers and surfers will find winds on the Atlantic coast are stronger in summer, but the swell is bigger in winter.

Desert and pre-desert areas are mostly dry and hot but, from December to February, are also extremely cold at night. On the other hand, mountain areas can get quite hot during the summer days. Occasional but heavy showers occur, turning dry riverbeds into dangerous flash floods, while snow blocks the passes of the High Atlas in winter.

Getting to Marrakech, High Atlas and Essaouira

Air
Major European airlines run frequent scheduled flights to Morocco's main airports at Marrakech, Casablanca-Mohammed V and Agadir, with most flights operating from France and Spain. National carrier **Royal Air Maroc (RAM)** (www.royalairmaroc.com) is reliable. Prices are similar to **Air France** and **British Airways**. The cheapest flights are usually with budget airlines **EasyJet**, **Ryanair** and **Atlas Blue**. Charter flights are another possible cheap option; run by package holiday companies, they fly mainly to Agadir. For information on **Aéroport Marrakech Menara**, see page 26.

Fly-boat It is possible to get a flight to Gibraltar, Almería or Málaga, and then continue by boat to Ceuta or Tangier in northwest Morocco, or Melilla or Nador further east (see Ferry, below).

Ferry
Shortest ferry crossings from Europe to Morocco are from Tarifa, Algeciras or Gibraltar to Tangier or Ceuta. Longer crossings run from Almería and Sète, France, to Melilla and Nador. Ceuta and Melilla are Spanish enclaves so you cross a land border in Africa. Algeciras to Ceuta is fast but the advantage is lost at the Fnideq land border crossing into Morocco. Algeciras to Tangier is the most convenient crossing, Tangier being the northernmost point on the Moroccan rail network and (almost) the starting point of the autoroute down to Casa-Rabat. In the summer months, those with cars will find ferries booked solid months in advance, as Moroccans working in Europe return home to visit family.

When you leave Spain for Morocco, your passport is checked by the Spanish authorities before boarding. Moroccan border formalities are undertaken on board: you fill in a disembarkation form and have your passport stamped at a *guichet*, generally as you get on board. Leaving Morocco, you fill in an embarkation form and departure card, which are stamped by the port police before getting on the boat. (Various people will offer to sell you the police *fiches* but they can be found free when you check in.) When you travel from Spain to Spanish enclaves Ceuta and Melilla, this does not apply.

Websites providing details of services (boats and hydrofoils) include **www.tras mediterranea.es** and **www.frs.es**.

Train

Train travel to Morocco is a relatively cheap option and a convenient way to tie in a visit to Morocco with a short stay in Europe, though Interrail tickets are no longer valid in the country. **ONCF** Moroccan rail services can be checked on www.oncf.ma.

Transport in Marrakech, High Atlas and Essaouira

When planning a trip in Morocco, remember that the distances are great and that long trips on buses can be tiring. Bus journeys are often excruciatingly slow, even over relatively short distances. To make maximum use of your time, especially if you don't mind dozing on a bus, take night buses to cover the longer distances. If you have sufficient funds, then there is always the option of internal flights – although these may not always fit in with your schedule. Public transport is reasonably priced, and the train network is good and being heavily invested in, although it doesn't cover the whole country. Car hire can be expensive; although you may be able to get a small car for 1800-2500dh a week, you still have petrol or diesel costs on top of this. In many places, however, a car enables you to reach places which are otherwise inaccessible.

Bicycles and motorcycles

Mountain bikes, mopeds and sometimes small motorcycles can be hired in tourist towns. There is no shortage of mechanics to fix bikes and mopeds. Trains, buses and even *grands taxis* will take bikes for a small fee. Some European companies now run cycling holidays, with bikes being carried on vans on the longer stretches.

If you go touring with a bike or motorcycle, beware of the sun. Wear gloves and cover those bits of exposed skin between helmet and T-shirt. For motorcyclists, helmets are complusory, and *gendarmes* will be happy to remind you of the fact.

Riding a motorbike in Morocco is even more testing than driving a car. Watch out for stray pedestrians and note that vehicle drivers will not show you much respect. Where flocks of animals are straying across the road, try not to drive between a single animal and the rest of the flock, as it may well try to charge back to join the rest. Use your horn. If you are going to go off-road, wear boots and make sure your tyres are in tiptop condition.

Theft from bicycle paniers is a problem. Anything loosely attached to your bike will disappear when you are being besieged by a horde of children in an isolated village.

Bus

Domestic bus services are plentiful. Price variations are small, while the quality of service varies enormously. Broadly speaking, if the train, a **Supratours** bus or a *grand taxi* run to your destination, don't bother with the small bus companies. For early morning services it's worth getting your ticket in advance, also at peak times when many Moroccans are travelling, such as the end of Ramadan and around Aïd el Kebir (two months after the end of Ramadan). You will find that there is a man who helps stow luggage on the roof or in the hold, so have a couple of dirham coins handy for him.

In southern Morocco, the safest and most comfortable service is also with Supratours. Next best is the **CTM**, Compagnie de transport marocain (white buses with blue and red stripes). Often (but not always) their services run from stations away from the main *gare routière* (inter-city bus station). This is the case in Marrakech, for example. For information (*renseignements*) on CTM services, try T0522-458881 or www.ctm.ma. Both Supratours and CTM buses usually run on time. As an example of prices, a single Marrakech to Essaouira costs 65dh with Supratours.

Safety Vehicles used by many private bus companies do not conform to high safety standards. Drivers are severely underpaid and, to make up for their low wages, may leave half-full, aiming to pick up extra passengers (whom they won't have to declare to their employers) en route. This makes for a slow, stop/go service. On routes worked by several companies, drivers race each other to be first to pick up passengers in the next settlement. Given the poor condition of the vehicles and the often narrow roads, accidents are inevitable.

City buses Most towns have city buses which provide great opportunities for local pickpockets when crowded. The orange **Alsa** buses in Marrakech are fine.

Car hire → *See also box, opposite.*

As distances are great, having a car makes a huge difference to the amount of ground you can cover. All the main hire car companies are represented and there are numerous small companies, which vary hugely in reliability. The Peugeot 205 is felt to be a more reliable small car, with slightly higher clearance and better road holding. A good deal would give you a Uno for 500dh a day, unlimited mileage, although some Marrakech agencies can be cheaper. 4WDs available in Morocco include the Suzuki Gemini (two people) and the Vitara (four people), at around 800dh per day; long-base Mitsubishi Pajeros (six people) are hired at 900-1000dh per day. Toyotas are said to be the best desert 4WDs. Landrovers are very uncomfortable for long cross-country runs on road, especially in summer without air conditioning. There is huge demand for hire cars during the Christmas and Easter breaks. Always try to have the mobile phone number of an agency representative in case of emergency. Many cars do not as yet use unleaded petrol – if you have one that does, you will find that not all petrol stations have unleaded, especially in the south. Always drive more slowly than you would in Europe.

Remember that you are responsible for damage if you take a car unsuited to the piste into areas suitable only for 4WDs. Regarding insurance, the best agencies will provide all risk insurance. Check for scratches and especially tyre condition (this includes spare tyre), presence of jack and warning triangle, working lights and safety belts. When hiring an

No rules of the road

Driving in Morocco is hazardous. *Grands taxis*, buses and lorries thunder along, forcing oncoming lesser vehicles on to the hard shoulder, if it exists. Sometimes there is a tyre-splitting gap between tarmac and dusty edge. Pedestrians wander out into the road and cyclists stray into the fast lane. On poor roads, you may see Moroccan drivers holding a palm up to their windscreens. This is to reduce the risk of shattering due to stones shooting up from the wheels of oncoming cars.

People also seem to overtake in the most suicidal of places. You can effectively buy yourself a driving licence in Morocco, and the accident figures are appalling: 25.6 deaths per 1000 accidents per year in Morocco, as against 2.6 deaths per 1000 accidents in France. The Gendarmerie royale is having a crackdown, however, especially on speed limits, and 400dh fines may be levied on the spot.

Do not rush, go with the flow and take your time. Apart from Casablanca, Morocco's cities are not large, and you will soon be out on the calmer country roads. Here you will share the roads with numerous animal-drawn carts and pack animals. This makes for slow driving but can also be dangerous at night. Most roads lack catseyes and most agricultural vehicles and mule carts drive without lights.

all-terrain vehicle, try to ascertain that the agency you are hiring from has a reliable, well-maintained fleet. Make sure that the vehicle will go into four-wheel drive easily.

In general, you will need dirhams to pay, as only the larger agencies take credit cards. They will take an imprint of your credit card as a guarantee. See individual city and town listings for details of companies.

Risky roads There are a number of dangerous stretches of road which you may have to deal with in your hire car. Much concentration is needed on the four-hour drive on the winding, mountainous N9, Marrakech to Ouarzazate, via the Tizi-n-Tichka. Fog and icy surfaces are possible in winter. There are roads which seem excellent, you drive fast and then meet sudden dips and turns, such as Ouarzazate to Skoura, Agdz to Nekob. In the Middle and High Atlas barriers are put across the road on routes to Azrou, Ifrane, Midelt and over the Tizi-n-Tichka and Tizi-n-Test when snow blocks roads.

Car parking In towns, parking is fairly easy. Parking meters rarely function, and instead a sort of watchman, identified by blue overalls and a metal badge will pop up. Give him some spare change, say 10dh, when you return to your undamaged vehicle. At night, it is essential to leave your vehicle in a place where there is a night watchman (*le gardien de nuit*). All good hotels and streets with restaurants will have such a figure who will keep an eye out.

Taxi

Long-distance *grands taxis*, generally Mercedes 200 saloon cars, run over fixed routes between cities, or within urban areas between the centre and outlying suburbs. There is a fixed price for each route and passengers pay for a place, six in a Mercedes, nine in a Peugeot 504 estate car. Taxis wait until they are full. You may, however, feel rich enough to pay for two places in order to be comfortable at the front (and be able to wear a safety belt). In a Peugeot estate, the best places are undoubtedly at the front, or, if you are quite small, right at the back. The middle place in the middle row is probably the worst.

Between towns, *grands taxis* are quicker than trains or buses and, normally, only a little more expensive. Each town has a rank for *grands taxis*, generally, although not always, next to the main bus station. The drivers cry out the name of their destination and, as you near the taxi station, you may be approached by touts eager to help you find a taxi.

In mountain areas, the same system applies, although the vehicles are Mercedes transit vans (where there is tarmac) or Landrovers, which have two people next to the driver and 10 in the back.

Petits taxis are used within towns and are generally Fiat Unos and Palios. They are colour-coded by town (blue for Rabat, red for Casa, khaki for Marrakech, tasteful pistachio green in Mohammedia). Officially they are metered, with an initial minimum fare, followed by increments of time and distance. There is a 50% surcharge after 2100. A *petit taxi* may take up to three passengers. In Marrakech, Rabat and Casablanca, drivers generally use the meters. Taxi drivers welcome a tip – many of them are not driving their own vehicles and make little more than 100dh a day. In terms of price, a short run between old and new town in Marrakech will set you back 12dh.

Where to stay in Marrakech, High Atlas and Essaouira

Morocco has a good range of accommodation to suit all budgets. There are several well-appointed business hotels in the main cities, luxurious places for the discerning visitor and clean basic hotels to suit those with limited funds. Independent travellers appreciate the growing number of *maisons d'hôte* or guesthouses (generally referred to as riads, see box, page 48), some very swish indeed, while, in the mountain areas, walkers and climbers will find rooms available in local people's homes. Modern self-catering accommodation is also sometimes available.

There is an official star rating system, although few hotels will boast about their membership of the one-, two- or even three-star categories. There does not appear to be very tight central control on how prices reflect facilities on offer. There are considerable variations in standards, and surprises are possible. Note, too, that breakfast is often not included in the room price – except in riads.

Cheap
At the budget end of the market are simple hotels, often close to bus or train stations. There may be a washbasin, sometimes a bidet. Loos and showers will usually be shared and you may have to pay for a hot shower. The worst of this sort of accommodation will be little better than a concrete cell, stifling in summer. The best is often quite pleasant outside summer, with helpful staff and lots of clean, bright tiling. Rooms often open on to a central courtyard, limiting privacy and meaning you have to leave your room closed when out. Outside the big tourist cities, such hotels have almost exclusively Moroccan customers. Although such hotels are generally clean, it may be best to bring a sheet with you if you're planning to use them a lot. Water, especially in the southern desert towns, can be a problem. Generally, there will be a public bath (hammam) close by for you to take a shower after a long bus journey.

Mid-range
More expensive one-star type hotels are generally in the new part of town (*ville nouvelle* neighbourhoods). Showers may be en suite, breakfast (coffee, bread and jam, a croissant, orange juice) should be available, possibly at the café on the ground floor, for around 20dh. Next up are the two- and three-star places. Most will be in the *ville nouvelle* areas of towns.

Price codes

Where to stay

€€€€ over €140   €€€ €71-140

€€ €35-70   € under €35

Prices are for double rooms. Singles are marginally cheaper. See page 21 for exchange rates.

Restaurants

€€€ over €30   €€ €15-30   € under €15

Price codes are for a two-course meal for one person, excluding drinks or service charge.

Rooms will have high ceilings and en suite shower and toilet. Light sleepers need to watch out for noisy, street-facing rooms. Some of these hotels are being revamped, not always very effectively. In this price bracket are a number of establishments with a personal, family-run feel.

Expensive

Top hotels are generally run by international groups, such as Accor and Le Méridien. Upmarket hotels in Morocco can either be vast and brash, revamped and nouveau riche, or solid but tasteful and even discreet with a touch of old-fashioned elegance. The main cities also have large business hotels.

Riads and guesthouses

The big phenomenon of the late 1990s and 2000s in the Moroccan tourist industry has been the development of the guesthouse. Wealthy Europeans have bought old property in the medinas of Marrakech, Fès and Essaouira as second homes. Rather than leave the property closed for much of the year, the solution was to rent it out. See box, page 48.

Youth hostels (Auberges de jeunesse)

There are 11 hostels in all affiliated to HI, located in the cities (Casablanca, Rabat, Fès, Meknès and Marrakech, Oujda and Laâyoune) as well as Azrou (Middle Atlas) and Asni (High Atlas). Overnight charges are 20-40dh, with use of the kitchen 2dh. There is a maximum stay of three nights and priority is given to the under-30s. For information try the **Moroccan Youth Hostel Federation**, Parc de la Ligue arabe, Casablanca, T0522-220551. It is often better to go for cheap hotels, more conveniently located and with better toilets and showers. The Marrakech hostel is located in the *ville nouvelle*, convenient for the train station, but a long way from sights and old-town atmosphere.

Mountain accommodation

In the mountains, you can easily bivouac out in summer or, in the high mountains, sleep in a stone *azib* (shepherd's shelter). There are three main options for paid accommodation: floor space in someone's home, a gîte of some kind, or a refuge run by the **CAF** (Club Alpin Français). The refuges are shelters with basic dormitory and kitchen facilities. Rates depend on category and season but about 15-50dh per night per person is usual. The CAF can also be contacted via BP 6178, Casablanca, T0522-270090, and BP 4437, Rabat, T0537-734442.

In remote villages, there are *gîtes d'étape*, simple dormitory accommodation, marked with the colourful **GTAM** (Grande traversée de l'Atlas marocain) logo. The warden generally

Hammams

A ritual purification of the body is essential before Muslims can perform prayers and, in the days before bathrooms, the 'major ablutions' were generally done at the hammam (bath). Segregation of the sexes is, of course, the rule at the hammam. Some establishments are only open for women, others are only for men, most have a shift system (mornings and evenings for the men, all afternoon for women). In the old days, the hammam, along with the local *zaouïa* or saint's shrine, was an important place for women to gather and socialize, and even pick out a potential wife for a son.

Very often there are separate hammams for men and women next to each other on the ground floor of an apartment building. A passage leads into a large changing room/post-bath area, equipped with masonry benches for lounging on and (sometimes) small wooden lockers. Here you undress under a towel. Hammam gear today is usually shorts for men and knickers for women. If you're going to have a massage/scrub down, you take a token at the cash desk where shampoo can also be bought.

The next step is to proceed to the hot room: five to 10 minutes with your feet in a bucket of hot water will have you sweating nicely and you can then move back to the raised area where the masseurs are at work. After the expert removal of large quantities of dead skin, you go into one of the small cabins or *mathara* to finish washing. (Before doing this, find the person bringing in dry towels so that they can bring yours to you when you're in the *mathara*.) For women, in addition to a scrub and a wash there may be the pleasures of epilation with *sokar*, a mix of caramelized sugar and lemon. Men can undergo a *taksira*, which involves much pulling and stretching of the limbs. And remember, allow plenty of time to cool down, reclining in the changing area.

Hotel hammams include **Riad El Fenn**, see page 45, with a *gommage* treatment that ends with two halves of a fresh orange being squeezed over your body and a jar of wonderful-smelling rosewater being poured over your head and face. The hammam at the funky **Riad El Cadi**, see page 47, has a small solar-heated pool and a jacuzzi you can dip into afterwards. Richard Branson's **Kasbah Tamadot**, see page 93, in Asni, has a hammam a few steps away from a lovely dark blue swimming pool.

lives in the house next door. Prices here are set by the **ONMT** (tourist board), and the gîte will be clean if spartan. The board also publishes an annual guide listing people authorized to provide gîte-type accommodation.

In mountain villages where there is no gîte, you will usually find space in people's homes, provided you have a sleeping bag. Many houses have large living rooms with room for people to bed down on thin foam mattresses. It is the custom to leave a small sum in payment for this sort of service. On the whole, you will be made very welcome.

Camping

There are campsites all over Morocco – the **ONMT** quotes 87 sites in well-chosen locations. Few sites, however, respect basic international standards. Security is a problem close to large towns, even if the site is surrounded by a wall with broken glass on top. Never leave anything valuable in your tent. Many campsites also lack shade, can be noisy and the ground tends to be hard and stony, requiring tough tent pegs. As campsites are really not much cheaper than basic hotels and, as even simple things like clean toilets and running water can be problematic, hotel accommodation is usually preferable. There are some notable exceptions however (see listings throughout the book).

Food and drink in Marrakech, High Atlas and Essaouira

Moroccan cuisine

The finest of the Moroccan arts is possibly its cuisine. There are the basics: harira and bessera soups, kebabs, couscous, tagine and the famous *pastilla*: pigeon, egg and almonds in layers of filo pastry. And there are other dishes, less well known: gazelle's horns, coiling m'hencha and other fabulous pastries. The Moroccans consider their traditional cooking to be on a par with Indian, Chinese and French cuisine – though the finest dishes are probably to be found in private homes. Today, however, upmarket restaurants, notably in Marrakech, will give you an idea of how good fine Moroccan food can be. Moroccan cuisine is beginning to get the international respect it deserves, with new restaurants opening in European capitals. However, the spices and vegetables, meat and fish, fresh from the markets of Morocco, give the edge to cooks in old medina houses.

The climate and soils of Morocco mean that magnificent vegetables can be produced all year round, thanks to assiduous irrigation. Although there is industrial chicken production, in many smaller restaurants, the chicken you eat is as likely to have been reared by a smallholder. Beef and lamb come straight from the local farms.

In addition to the basic products, Moroccan cooking gets its characteristic flavours from a range of spices and minor ingredients. Saffron (*zaâfrane*), though expensive, is widely used, turmeric (*kurkum*) is also much in evidence. Other widely used condiments include a mixed all spice, referred to as *ra's el hanout* ('head of the shop'), cumin (*kamoun*), black pepper, oregano and rosemary (*yazir*). Prominent greens in use include broad-leaved parsley (*ma'dnous*), coriander (*kuzbur*) and, in some variations of couscous, a sort of celery called *klefs*. Preserved lemons (modestly called *bouserra*, 'navels', despite their breast-like shape) can be found in fish and chicken tagines. Bay leaves (*warqa Sidna Moussa*, 'the leaf of our lord Moses') are also commonly employed. Almonds, much used in pâtisserie, are used in tagines too, while powdered cinnamon (Arabic *karfa*, *cannelle* in French) provides the finishing touch for *pastilla*. In pâtisserie, orange-flower water and rose water (*ma ouarda*) are essential to achieve a refined taste.

Eating times vary widely in Morocco. Marrakech gets up early – and goes to bed early, too, so people tend to sit down to dine around about 2000. Across the country, the big meal of the week is Friday lunch, a time for people to gather in their families. The main meal of the day tends to be lunch, although this varies according to work and lifestyle. As anywhere, eating out in plush eateries is a popular upper-income occupation. Locals will tend to favour restaurants with French or southern European cuisine, while Moroccan 'palace' restaurants are patronized almost exclusively by tourists.

Starters *Harira* is a basic Moroccan soup; ingredients vary but include chick peas, lentils, veg and a little meat. Often eaten accompanied with hard-boiled eggs. *Bissara* is a pea soup, a cheap and filling winter breakfast. *Briouat* are tiny envelopes of filo pastry, akin to the Indian samosa, with a variety of savoury fillings. They also come with an almond filling for dessert.

Snacks Cheaper restaurants serve kebabs (aka *brochettes*), with tiny pieces of beef, lamb and fat. Also popular is *kefta*, mince-meat brochettes, served in sandwiches with chips, mustard and *harissa* (red-pepper spicy sauce). Tiny bowls of finely chopped tomato and onion are another popular accompaniment. On Jemaâ el Fna in Marrakech, strong stomachs may want to snack on the local *babouche* (snails).

Main dishes *Seksou* (couscous) is the great North African speciality. Granules of semolina are steamed over a pot filled with a rich meat and vegetable stew. Unlike Tunisian couscous, which tends to be flavoured with a tomato sauce, Moroccan couscous is pale yellow. In some families, couscous is the big Friday lunch.

Tagines are stews, the basic Moroccan dish. It is actually the term for the two-part terracotta dish (base and conical lid) in which meat or fish are cooked with a variety of vegetables, essentially, carrots, potato, onion and turnip. Tagine is everywhere in Morocco. Simmered in front of you on a *brasero* at a roadside café, it is always good and safe to eat. Out trekking it is the staple of life. For tagines, there are four main sauce preparations: *m'qalli*, a yellow sauce created using olive oil, ginger and saffron; *m'hammer*, a red sauce which includes butter, paprika (*felfla hlwa*) and cumin; *qudra*, another yellow sauce, slightly lighter than *m'qalli*, made using butter, onions, pepper and saffron, and finally *m'chermel*, made using ingredients from the other sauces. Variations on these base sauces are obtained using a range of ingredients, including parsley and coriander, garlic and lemon juice, *boussera*, eggs, sugar, honey and cinnamon (*karfa*).

In the better restaurants, look out for *djaj bil-hamid* (chicken with preserved lemons and olives), sweet and sour *tajine barkouk* (lamb with plums), *djaj qudra* (chicken with almonds and caramelized onion) and *tajine maqfoul*. Another tasty dish is *tajine kefta*, basically fried minced meat balls cooked with eggs and chopped parsley. In eateries next to food markets, delicacies such as *ra's embekhar* (steamed sheep's head) and *kourayn* (animal feet) are popular.

A dish rarely prepared in restaurants is *djaj souiri*, aka *djaj mqeddem*, the only *plat gratiné* in Moroccan cuisine. Here, at the very last minute, a sauce of beaten eggs and chopped parsley is added to the chicken, already slow-cooked in olives, diced preserved lemon, olive oil and various spices.

All over Morocco, lamb is much appreciated, and connoisseurs reckon they can tell what the sheep has been eating (rosemary, mountain pasture, straw, or mixed rubbish at the vast Mediouna tip near Casablanca). Lamb is cheaper in drought years, when farmers have to reduce their flocks, expensive when the grazing is good, and is often best eaten at roadside restaurants where the lorry drivers pull in for a feed.

Desserts A limited selection of desserts is served in Moroccan restaurants. In the palace restaurants, there will be a choice between *orange à la cannelle* (slices of orange with cinnamon) or some sort of marzipan pâtisserie like *cornes de gazelle* or *ghrayeb*, rather like round short-cake. *El jaouhar*, also onomatopoeically known as *tchak-tchouka*, is served as a pile of crunchy, fried filo pastry discs topped with a sweet custardy sauce with almonds. Also on offer you may find *m'hencha*, coils of almond paste wrapped in filo pastry, served crisp from the oven and sprinkled with icing sugar and cinnamon, and *bechkito*, little crackly biscuits.

Most large towns will have a couple of large pâtisseries, providing French pastries and the petits fours essential for proper entertaining. See **Pâtisserie Hilton**, Rue de Yougoslavie, Marrakech. Here you will find *slilou* (aka *masfouf*), a richly flavoured nutty powder served in tiny saucers to accompany tea but you won't find *maâjoun*, the Moroccan equivalent of hash brownies, made to liven up dull guests at wedding parties.

In local *laiteries*, try a glass of yoghurt. Oranges (*limoun*) and mandarins (*tchina*) are cheap, as are prickly pears, sold off barrows. In winter, in the mountains, look out for kids selling tiny red arbutus berries (*sasnou*) carefully packaged in little wicker cones. Fresh hazelnuts are charmingly known as *tigerguist*.

Dishes for Ramadan At sunset the fast is broken with a rich and savoury *harira* (see above), *beghrira* (little honeycombed pancakes served with melted butter and honey) and *shebbakia* (lace-work pastry basted in oil and covered in honey). Distinctive too are the sticky pastry whorls with sesame seeds on top.

Cafés and restaurants

Cafés offer croissants, petit-pain and cake (Madeleine), occasionally soup and basic snacks. Restaurants basically divide into four types: snack eateries, in the medina and *ville nouvelle*, are generally cheap and basic. Some are modelled on international themed fast-food restaurants. Then you have the *laiteries*, which sell yoghurt, fruit juices and will make up sandwiches with processed cheese, salad and *kacher* (processed meat). Full-blown restaurants are generally found only in larger towns, and some are very good indeed. And, finally, in cities like Marrakech, you have the great palaces of Moroccan cuisine, restaurants set in old, often beautifully restored private homes. These can set you back 500dh or even more. Some of these restaurants allow you to eat à la carte (**El Fassia** in Marrakech), rather than giving you the full banquet menu (and late-night indigestion).

Eating out cheaply If you're on a very tight budget, try the ubiquitous food stalls and open-air restaurants serving various types of soup, normally the standard broth (*harira*), snacks and grilled meat. The best place for the adventurous open-air eater is the Jemaâ el Fna square in Marrakech. Another good place is the fish market in the centre of Essaouira. There is a greater risk of food poisoning at street eateries, so go for food that is cooked as you wait, or that is on the boil. Avoid fried fish that is already cooked and is reheated when you order it.

Vegetarian food Moroccan food is not terribly interesting for vegetarians, and in many places 'vegetarian cuisine' means taking the meat off the top of the couscous or tagine. The concept is really quite alien to most Moroccans, as receiving someone well for dinner means serving them a tagine with good chunk of meat. There are some excellent salads, however. Be prepared to eat lots of processed cheese and omelettes.

Food markets Each city has a colourful central market, generally dating back to the early years of the 20th century, stuffed with high-quality fresh produce. Try the Guéliz market in Marrakech, on the Avenue Mohammed V, on your left after the intersection with Rue de la Liberté as you head for the town centre.

Eating in people's homes Moroccan families may eat from a communal dish, often with spoons, sometimes with the hands. If invited to a home, you may well be something of a guest of honour. Depending on your hosts, it's a good idea to take some fruit or pâtisseries along. If spoons or cutlery are not provided, you eat using bread, using your right hand, not the left hand since it is ritually unclean. If the dishes with the food are placed at floor level, keep your feet tucked under your body away from the food. In a poorer home, there will only be a small amount of meat, so wait until a share is offered. Basically, good manners are the same anywhere. Let common sense guide you.

Drink

Tea All over Morocco the main drink apart from water is mint tea (*thé à la menthe/attay*) a cheap, refreshing drink which is made with green tea, fresh mint and masses of white sugar. The latter two ingredients predominate in the taste. If you want a reduced sugar tea, ask for *attay msous* or *bila sukar/sans sucre*). In cafés, tea is served in mini-metal tea pots, poured from high above the glass to generate a froth (*attay bi-rizatou*, 'tea with a turban') to use the local expression. Generally, tradition has it that you drink three glasses. To avoid burning your fingers, hold the glass with thumb under the base and index finger on rim. In some homes, various other herbs are added to make a more interesting brew, including *flayou* (peppermint), *louiza* (verbena) and even *sheeba* (absinthe). If you want a herb tea, ask for a *verveine* or *louiza*, which may be with either hot water or hot milk (*bil-halib*).

Coffee Coffee is commonly drunk black and strong (*kahwa kahla/un exprès*). For a weak milky coffee, ask for a *café au lait/kahwa halib*. A stronger milky coffee is called a *café cassé/kahwa mherza*.

Other soft drinks All the usual soft drinks are available in Morocco. If you want still mineral water (*eau plate*) ask for Sidi Harazem, Sidi Ali or Ciel. The main brands of fizzy mineral water (*eau pétillante*), are Oulmès and Bonacqua, a water produced by Coca Cola.
The better cafés and local *laiteries* (milk-product shops) do milkshakes, combinations of avocado, banana, apple and orange, made to measure. Ask for a *jus d'avocat* or a *jus de banane*, for example, or for a usually excellent lucky dip, a *jus mixte*.

Wines and spirits For a Muslim country, Morocco is fairly relaxed about alcohol. In the top hotels, imported spirits are available, although at a price. The main locally made lager **beers** are Flag, Flag Spécial, Stork, Castel and Heineken. In the spring, look out for the extremely good Bière de Mars, made only in March with Fès spring water.
Morocco produces **wine**, the main growing areas being Guerrouane and Meknès. Reds tend to prevail. **Celliers de Meknès** (CdM) and **Sincomar** are the main producers. At the top of the scale (off-licence prices in brackets), are Médaillon (90dh) and Beau Vallon (CdM, 90dh, anything up to 185dh in a restaurant). A CdM Merlot will set you back 45dh. Another reliable red is Domaine de Sahari, Aït Yazem, a pleasant claret, best drunk chilled in summer (30dh). The whites include Coquillages and Sémillant, probably the best (40dh). At the very bottom of the scale is rough and ready Rabbi Jacob, or, cheaper and still cheerful, Chaud Soleil. The local fig firewater is Mahia la Gazelle.
If you want to buy alcohol outside a restaurant, every major town will have a few licensed sales points. Often they are very well stocked with local and imported wines. The **Marjane** hypermarket chain, in all the major cities, also has an off-licence section. **Asouak Essalam**, the main competitor, does not stock alcohol, however. In Ramadan, alcohol is on sale to non-Muslim foreigners only and many of the off-licences shut down for the month. At Marjane, towards the end of Ramadan, you may well be asked by locals to buy a few bottles for their end of fasting party.

Festivals in Marrakech, High Atlas and Essaouira

Morocco has a number of regional and local festivals, often focusing around a local saint or the harvest time of a particular product, and are fairly recent in origin. The *moussems*, or traditional local festivals, have on occasion been banned in recent years, the authorities giving as a reason the health risks created by gatherings of large numbers of people in places with only rudimentary sanitary facilities. The main Moroccan festivals come in 3 categories: firstly, the more religious festivals, the timing of which relates to the lunar Islamic year, see page 22; secondly the annual semi-commercial regional or town festivals with relatively fixed dates; and thirdly, the new generation of arts and film festivals.

Regional and festivals

May Les Alizés, Essaouira. Small classical music festival in early May, www.alizes festival.com.

Jun Festival of Folk Art and Music, Marrakech.

Festival Gnaoua, Essaouira. One of Morocco's most successful music festivals, www.festival-gnaoua.co.ma.

Aug Moussem of Setti Fatma, Setti Fatma, Ourika Valley near Marrakech.

Sep Moussem des Fiançailles (Marriage Festival), Allamghou, near Imilchil (see box, page 100).

Dec Festival international du film de Marrakech, Marrakech. Established annual film fest, www.festivalmarrakech.info.

Shopping in Marrakech, High Atlas and Essaouira

Morocco is a shopper's paradise. The famous souks in Marrakech, in particular, are a great place to buy souvenirs as well as experiencing the cut and thrust of haggling with the experts. Good items to buy in Marrakech include thuya wood boxes, painted wood mirrors, ceramics, leather bags and *babouches* (shoes/slippers) and wrought-iron mirror frames. The fashionable coastal town of Essaouira is also a good place to shop; objects made in fragrant, honey-brown thuya wood are everywhere, from small boxes inlaid with lemon-wood to chunky, rounded sculptures. See under each destination for more details and the best places to find these items.

Trekking in the High Atlas

There are considerable opportunities for walking in Morocco. The most popular area is the **Toubkal National Park** in the High Atlas. However, as roads improve and inveterate trekkers return for further holidays, new areas are becoming popular. Starting in the west, to the south of the High Atlas, the **Jbel Siroua**, east of Taroudant, is a plateau with pleasant spring walking. The **Western High Atlas**, page 84, is best from late April to October, with various loops up into the mountains. You will probably want to climb North Africa's highest peak, Jbel Toubkal (4167 m); the only problem is that the mountain has become almost too popular. South of Azilal, the beautiful **Vallée des Aït Bougmez**, page 99, is also becoming popular. For weekend trekkers, there are gentle walks along the flat valley bottom but the Aït Bougmez also makes a good departure point for tougher treks, including the north–south crossing of the west-central High Atlas to Bou Thraghar, near Boumalne and El Kelaâ des Mgouna. On this route, you have the chance to climb the region's second highest peak, **Irhil Mgoun** (4071 m).

The **Middle Atlas** is much less well known to walkers. Certain parts are quite a Hobbit land, especially between Azrou, and the source of the Oum er Rabi river, where there is beautiful walking in the cedar forests. Despite its proximity to the rich farmlands of Meknès and the Saïs Plain, this is an extremely poor region that would benefit from increased ecologically friendly tourism.

The best time of year for walking is April to October; in the high summer keep to the high valleys, which are cooler and where water can be obtained. Views are not as good in the High Atlas at the height of summer because of the haze. Camping or bivouacking is fine in summer but in autumn indoor accommodation is necessary, in refuges, shepherds' huts or local homes. The use of mules or donkeys to carry the heavy packs is common.

To organize your trip, you can either book through a specialist trekking operator in your home country or hope to find a guide available when you arrive. In popular trekking areas, such as Toubkal, guides can fairly easily be found in trailhead settlements.

Specialist maps and walking guides are useful but can be hard to find in Morocco. You may be able to buy some at the **Hotel Ali** in Marrakech. Classified guest rooms in rural areas now have the **GTAM** (Grande Traversée des Atlas Marocains) label of approval. Places where trekking guides can be arranged include: Hotel Ali in Marrakech (High Atlas); Auberge Timnay near Midelt (Middle Atlas and Jbel Ayyachi); and Auberge Souktana, Taliouine, near Taroudant (for Jbel Siroua).

If you are setting up a trek yourself, note that a good mule can carry up to 100 kg (approximately three rucksacks). A mule with a muleteer costs around 120dh per day; a good guide should be paid 250dh per day, a cook around 150dh. When buying food for the trek with your guide, you will have to buy enough for the muleteers, too. Generally, trekkers will consume about 100dh worth of food and soft drinks a day. If you do a linear trek rather than a loop, you will generally have to pay for the 'mule-days' it takes to get the pack animals back to their home village.

In order to fully appreciate the beauty of the Atlas, trekkers need to ensure that the walking is as comfortable as possible, and this includes finding ways to deal with dehydration and fatigue. As on any hill trek, a steady, regular pace should be maintained. A good trip leader will ensure you make an early start, to enjoy walking in the cool mornings. Vehicle pistes look alluring to walk on but are in fact hard on the feet. Keep to the softer edges or go for footpaths when possible. Gorges are not the easiest places to walk in, so your local guide should know of the higher routes, if there is one that is safe. Pay particular attention if your route involves some scree running; you don't want to leave the mountains on a mule because of a sprained ankle. If you are not used to walking at altitude, try to avoid high routes in the early stages of your trip. Ensure you pause if a dizzy feeling sets in. In villages that see a lot of tourists children will be on the lookout, ready to scrounge a dirham or a 'bonbon'. They may be useful in showing you the way through to the footpath on the other side of the settlement.

There are a few books on trek routes in English. Alan Palmer's *Moroccan Atlas* trekking guide (Trailblazer, 2010) has 44 trail maps; Des Clark's *Mountaineering in the Moroccan High Atlas* (Cicerone, 2011) concentrates on winter walking for the experienced mountaineer, covering 40 peaks over 3000 m. Experienced Atlas walker Hamish M Brown's new *The High Atlas* (Cicerone, 2012), covers 48 routes, details the area's culture and offers practical guidance.

You can also contact the **Royal Moroccan Federation of Skiing and Mountaineering**, Parc de la Ligue Arabe, Casablanca, T0522-203798.

Essentials A-Z

Accident and emergency

Police: T19. **Fire brigade**: T15. Larger towns will have an **SOS Médecins** (private doctor on-call service) and almost all towns of any size have a pharmacy on duty at night, the *pharmacie de garde*. Any large hotel should be able to give you the telephone/address of these. For most ailments, a *médecin généraliste* (GP) will be sufficient.

Dress

In coastal resorts, you can wear shorts and expose arms and shoulders. However, when wandering round medinas and going to city centres, both men and women should cover shoulders. Sandals are fine but shorts should be baggy not skimpy. Expect lots of remarks and attention if you do go wandering round the souks in your running shorts. Have some smart but cool tops with you for summer travelling. Inland, winter is cold. Night temperatures in the desert and at altitude are low all the year – a fleece is handy, even as a pillow.

Electricity

Morocco has a fairly reliable electricity supply of 220V, using continental European round 2-pin plugs. In some more remote areas, however, there is no mains electricity.

Embassies and consulates

For all Moroccan embassies and consulates abroad and for all foreign embassies and consulates in Morocco, see http://embassy.goabroad.com.

Health

No vaccinations are required unless you're travelling from a country where yellow fever and/or cholera frequently occurs. You should be up to date with **polio**, **tetanus**, and **typhoid** protection. If you are going to be travelling in rural areas where hygiene is often a bit rough and ready, then having a **hepatitis B** shot is a good thing. You could also have a **cholera** shot, although there is no agreement among medics on how effective this is.

Major health risks include acute **mountain sickness**, which can strike from about 3000 m upwards and, in general, is more likely to affect those who ascend rapidly (for example by plane) and those who over-exert themselves. Acute mountain sickness takes a few hours or days to come on and presents with headache, lassitude, dizziness, loss of appetite, nausea and vomiting. When trekking to high altitude, some time spent walking at medium altitude, getting fit and acclimatizing is beneficial.

Some form of **diarrhoea** or intestinal upset is almost inevitable; the standard advice is to be careful with drinking water and ice; if you have any doubts about the water then boil it or filter and treat it. In a restaurant, buy bottled water or ask where the water has come from. Food can also pose a problem; be wary of salads if you don't know whether they have been washed or not. In major cities, tap water should be fine to drink, though many visitors stick to bottled water to make sure. Out in the sticks you should definitely only drink the bottled variety.

There is a very minimal risk of **malaria** in Morocco and usually prophylaxis is not advised but check before you go. If you are going to be travelling in remote parts of the Saharan provinces, then a course of malaria tablets may be recommended.

A **rabies** vaccination before travel can be considered but, if bitten, always seek urgent medical attention – whether or not you have been previously vaccinated – after first cleaning the wound and treating with an iodine-base disinfectant or alcohol.

Further information

Foreign and Commonwealth Office (FCO) (UK), www.fco.gov.uk.
National Travel Health Network and Centre (NaTHNaC), www.nathnac.org.
World Health Organisation, www.who.int.
Fit for Travel (UK), www.fitfortravel.nhs.uk.
A-Z of vaccine and travel health advice requirements for each country.

Language

Arabic is the official language of Morocco, but nearly all Moroccans with a secondary education have enough French to communicate with, and a smattering of English. In the North, Spanish maintains a presence thanks to TV and radio. Outside education, however, Moroccan Arabic in the cities and Amazigh in the mountains are the languages of everyday life, and attempts to use a few words and phrases, no matter how stumblingly, will be appreciated. Those with some Arabic learned elsewhere often find Moroccan Arabic difficult. It is characterized by a clipped quality (the vowels just seem to disappear), and the words taken from classical Arabic are often very different from those used in the Middle East. In addition, there is the influence of the Berber languages and a mixture of French and Spanish terms, often heavily 'Moroccanized'. In many situations French is more or less understood. However, you will come across plenty of people who have had little opportunity to go to school and whose French may be limited to a very small number of phrases.

If you wish to learn Arabic, **ALIF** (Arabic Language Institute in Fès, T0535-624850, www.alif-fes.com), an offshoot of the American Language Centre, has a very good reputation. They organize a range of long and short courses in both classical and Moroccan Arabic. Courses in Amazigh languages can be set up, too.

See Footnotes, page 108, for lists of useful words and phrases.

Money
Currency

The major unit of currency in Morocco is the dirham (dh). In 1 dirham there are 100 centimes. There are coins for 1 centime (very rare), 5, 10, 20 and 50 centimes, and for 1, 2, 5 and 10 dirhams, as well as notes for 20, 50, 100 and 200 dirhams. The coins can be a little confusing. There are 2 sorts of 5 dirham coin: the older and larger cupro-nickel ('silver coloured' version), being phased out, and the new bi-metal version, brass colour on the inside. There is a brownish 20 dirham note, easily confused with the 100 dirham note. The 50 dirham note is green, the 100 dirham is brown and sand colour, and the 200 dirham note is in shades of blue and turquoise. Currency is labelled in Arabic and French.

You can sometimes buy Moroccan dirhams at bureaux de change at the London airports but dirhams may not be taken out of Morocco. If you have excess dirhams, you can exchange them back into euros at a bank on production of exchange receipts. However, as European cash and Visa cards function in Moroccan ATMs (*guichets automatiques*), in major towns it is possible to withdraw more or less exactly the amount you need on a daily basis. At weekends and during big public holidays, airport and city-centre ATMs can be temperamental. The most reliable ATMs are those of the **Wafa Bank** (green and yellow livery) and the **BMCI**.

Moroccans among themselves sometimes count in older currency units. To the confusion of travellers, many Moroccans refer to francs, which equal 1 centime, and reals, though both these units only exist in speech. Even more confusingly, the value of a real varies from region to region. A dirham equals 20 reals in most regions. However, around Tangier and in most of the North, 1 dirham equals 2 reals. Alf franc (1000 francs) is 10 dirhams. Unless you are good at calculations, it's easiest to stick to dirhams.

Exchange rate → US$1 = 8.8dh,
UK £1 = 13.8dh, €1 = 11dh (May 2012).
There is a fixed rate for changing notes and no commission ought to be charged for this.

Credit cards

Credit cards are widely accepted at banks, top hotels, restaurants and big tourist shops. For restaurants, check first before splashing out. Remember to keep all credit card receipts – and, before you sign, check where the decimal marker (a comma in Morocco rather than a dot) has been placed, and that there isn't a zero too many. You don't want to be paying thousands rather than hundreds of dirhams. To reduce problems with card fraud, it makes sense to use a credit card for payments of large items like carpets and hotel bills. If a payment is not legitimate, it is a lot less painful if the transaction is on the credit card rather than drawn from your current account.

Traveller's cheques

Although somewhat time-consuming to change, traveller's cheques (TCs) are still useful (though a small commission will be charged for changing them). Take TCs from a well-known bank or company, preferably in euros. Some hotels and shops will exchange TCs.

Banks

Main banks include the **BMCE, Crédit du Maroc, Wafabank** and **Banque Populaire**; all are widespread. The **BMCE** and the **Crédit du Maroc** seem to have the best change facilities, while the **Banque Populaire** is often the only bank in southern towns. Banking in Morocco can be a slow, tortuous process. The easiest way to get money is thus to use your credit or debit card at a cash dispenser. See Opening hours, below, for banking hours.

Cost of travelling

As a budget traveller, it is possible to get by in Morocco for £30-35/US$60-70 a day. Your costs can be reduced by having yoghurt and bread and cheese for lunch and staying in an 80dh a night hotel (you can often find even cheaper options in small towns).

Accommodation, food and transport are all relatively cheap compared to Europe and America, and there is a lot to see and do for free. However, this budget does not allow much room for unexpected costs like the frequent small tips expected for minor services. If you start buying imported goods, notably cosmetics and toiletries, foods and electrical goods, things can get expensive. Allowing £40/US$80 is more realistic.

In top-quality hotels, restaurants, nightclubs and bars, prices are similar to Europe. Rabat, Casablanca and Agadir are the most expensive places, while manufactured goods in remote rural areas tend to cost more. Around the 200dh mark, you can get a much better meal in a restaurant than you can in western Europe. Shoppers will be more than satisfied with the gifts on sale (prices negotiable). Prices for food and drink are non-negotiable.

Cost of living

Although prices for many basics can seem very low indeed to those used to prices in European capitals, the cost of living is high for most Moroccans. At one end of the scale, in the mountainous rural areas, there is Morocco's fourth world, still on the margins of the cash economy. In these regions, families produce much of their own food and are badly hit in drought years when there is nothing to sell in the souk to generate cash to buy oil, extra flour and sugar. This precariousness means much 'hidden' malnutrition.

Conditions are improving for the city shanty-town dwellers. Here, families will be getting by on 2000dh a month, sometimes much less. The urban middle classes, those with salaried jobs in the public and private sectors, are doing fairly well. A primary school teacher may be on 3000dh a month; a private company employee at the start of their career will make around 3000dh a month, too. This category has access to loans and is seeing a general improvement in living standards. Morocco's top-flight IT technicians, doctors and business people have a plush lifestyle, with villas and servants, available to few Europeans. And, finally, a very small group of plutocrats has long been doing very, very well, thank you.

To put the contrasts in perspective, there are parents for whom the best option is to place their pre-adolescent girls as maids with city families in exchange for 300dh a month. The Amazigh-speaking boy who serves you in the corner shop may be given 50dh a week, plus food and lodging (of a sort). His horizons will be limited to the shop; there will be a trip back to the home village once a year; he may never learn to read. At the other, distant end of the scale, there are couples who can easily spend 40,000dh a semester to purchase an English-language higher education for one of their offspring at the private Al Akhawayn University in Ifrane.

Opening hours
The working week for businesses is Mon to Fri, with half-day working Sat. On Fri, the lunch break tends to be longer, as the main weekly prayers with sermon are on that day. Official business takes considerably longer in Ramadan.

Banks: 0830-1130 and 1430-1600 in winter; afternoons 1500-1700 in summer; 0930-1400 during Ramadan.

Museums: Most close on a Tue. Hours generally 0900-1200 and 1500-1700, although this can vary considerably.

Post offices: 0830-1230 and 1430-1830, shorter hours in Ramadan.

Shops: Generally 0900-1200 and 1500-1900, although this varies in the big towns.

Public holidays
1 Jan New Year's Day.
1 May Fête du Travail (Labour Day).
9 Jul Fête de la Jeunesse.
30 Jul Fête du Trône. Commemorates the present king Mohammed VI's accession.
20 Aug Anniversaire de la Révolution.
6 Nov Marche Verte/El Massira el Khadhra. Commemorates a march by Moroccan civilians to retake the Spanish-held Saharan territories of Río de Oro and Saguiet El Hamra.
18 Nov Independence Day. Commemorates independence and Mohammed V's return from exile.

Religious holidays
Religious holidays are scheduled according to the Hijna calendar, a lunar-based calendar. The lunar year is shorter than the solar year, so the Muslim year moves forward by 11 days every Christian year.
1 Muharram First day of the Muslim year.
Mouloud Celebration of the Prophet Mohammed's birthday.
Ramadan A month of fasting and sexual abstinence during daylight hours.
Aïd el Fitr (the Lesser Aïd) A 2-day holiday ending the month of Ramadan.
Aïd el Kebir (the Great Aïd) A 1-day holiday that comes 70 days after Aïd el Fitr. Commemorates how God rewarded Ibrahim's faith by sending down a lamb for him to sacrifice instead of his son. When possible, every family sacrifices a sheep on this occasion.

During **Ramadan**, the whole country switches to a different rhythm. Public offices open part time, and the general pace slows down during the daytime. No Moroccan would be caught eating in public during the day, and the vast majority of cafés and restaurants, except those frequented by resident Europeans and tourists, are closed. At night, the ambience is almost palpable.

There is a sense of collective effort, shared with millions of other Muslims worldwide. People who never go out all year are out visiting friends and family, strolling the streets in Ramadan. Shops stay open late, especially during the second half of the month. Ramadan is an interesting and frustrating time to visit Morocco as a tourist, but probably to be avoided if possible if you need to do business.

Safety

Morocco is basically a very safe country, although there is occasional violent street crime in Casablanca and (very rarely) Marrakech. Travelling on public transport, you need to watch your pockets. Do not carry all your money and cards, etc, in the same place. A money belt is a good idea. Never have more money than you can afford to lose in the pockets of your jeans. Thieves operate best in crowds, getting on and off trains and at bus and taxi stations where they can quickly disappear into an anonymous mass of people.

Be aware of the various skilled con-artists in operation in certain places. There are all sorts of ruses used by hasslers to extract a little money from tourists: 'the sick relative story', 'the *grand taxi* fare to Rabat to start university story', 'the supplement for the onward reservation to Chaouen story'. You need to be polite and confident, distant and sceptical and even a little bored by the whole thing. Learn the values of the banknotes quickly (the yellow-brown 100dh and the blue 200dh are the big ones, a red 10dh is no great loss). Keep your wits about you. Remember, you are especially vulnerable stumbling bleary-eyed off that overnight bus.

Should you be robbed, reporting it to the police will take time – but may alert them to the fact that there are thieves operating in a given place.

Security and terrorism

On the night of 14 May 2003, Casablanca was shaken by co-ordinated suicide bomb attacks targeting a Jewish social club and a major hotel. Over 40 Moroccans were murdered. Salafiya-Jihadiya fundamentalist groups organized these murders and the national security forces reacted with a wave of arrests. Summer 2003 saw the men responsible, including some of the suicide-bombers who survived, on trial. Nine of those found guilty escaped from prison in Kénitra in 2008.

After 2003, Morocco had seen little urban terrorism and violence until the Marrakech bombing of 2011.

The Moroccan government claims to have broken up 55 terrorist cells since 2003, and there are around 1000 Islamists in the country's jails on terrorist charges. There is tight monitoring of all fundamentalist activity and zero tolerance of anything which might lead to violence. As anything Jewish is an obvious target, there are police outside most synagogues.

Time

Morocco follows the UK all year round, with GMT in winter and GMT+1 in summer. Ceuta and Melilla work on Spanish time.

Tipping

This can be a bit of a 'hidden cost' during your stay in Morocco. Tipping is expected in restaurants and cafés, by guides, porters and car park attendants and others who render small services. Make sure you have small change at the ready. Tipping taxi drivers is optional. Do not tip for journeys when the meter has not been used, because the negotiated price will be generous anyway. For porters in hotels, tip around 3dh, on buses 3dh-5dh, and 5dh on trains and in airports.

Tourist information
Moroccan tourist boards abroad
For **Moroccan National Tourist
Board (ONMT)** locations worldwide,
see www.visitmorocco.org.

Morocco on the web
www.alif-fes.com For those wanting to
study Arabic and Amazigh languages.
www.emarrakech.info News of the Red
City, regularly updated but in French only.
www.lexicorient.com/morocco
Information on cities with photographs.
www.kelma.org French-based site with
news and views from the gay community
in the Maghreb, Belgium and France.
www.maroque.co.uk For design
inspiration.
www.north-africa.com Weekly analysis
on economics, politics and business.
Subscriber service.
www.riadzany.blogspot.com Titled 'The
View From Fez', this blog is actually a great
round-up of what's going on in Morocco
as a whole.

Visas
No visas are required for full passport
holders of the UK, USA, Canada, Australia,
New Zealand/Aotearoa, Canada, Ireland
and most EU countries. Benelux passport
holders require visas at the present time.
On the aeroplane or boat, or at the border,
travellers will be required to fill in a form
with standard personal and passport
details, an exercise to be repeated in almost
all hotels and guesthouses throughout the
country. From the point of entry, travellers
can stay in Morocco for 3 months.

Visa extensions
These require a visit to the Immigration or
Bureau des Etrangers department at the
police station of a larger town, as well as
considerable patience. An easier option is
to leave Morocco for a few days, preferably
to Spain or the Canary Islands, or to one
of the two Spanish enclaves, either Ceuta,
close to Tangier, or Melilla, rather more
remote in northeastern Morocco. People
coming into Morocco from either of these
Spanish enclaves for a second or third time
have on occasion run into problems with
the Moroccan customs. With numerous
foreigners resident in Agadir and Marrakech,
it may be easiest to arrange visa extensions
in these cities. Approval of the extension
has to come from Rabat and may take a
few days.

Weights and measures
Morocco uses the metric system.

Contents

Footprint features

Marrakech & Essaouira

Marrakech

Marrakech is Morocco's main point of entry for tourists, many of whom never venture far beyond its red walls, despite the enticing and dramatic backdrop of the High Atlas mountains, snow-capped until April or May and a venue for numerous excursions (see page 84). The city has a memorable beauty, with its palm-lined streets and red earth walls, surrounding a huge medina of flat-roofed houses. Above all, Marrakech is worth visiting to experience the vibrant mass of food stalls, musicians and snake charmers in the seething Jemaâ el Fna square, and for its souks – a labyrinthine network of markets, where people come to buy and sell from all over the surrounding plains, the High Atlas and the Sahara.

Arriving in Marrakech

Getting there

Accessible by air, road and rail, the city makes an excellent central point of arrival in Morocco, situated at the meeting point of routes for Essaouira (Atlantic coast), Ouarzazate (key to the gorges south of the Atlas and Sahara desert), and the northern imperial cities. **Airport Marrakech Menara** ① *T0524-447910, www.marrakech.airport-authority.com*, is 6 km west of the city, by the Menara Gardens. The number of passengers the airport handles has tripled over the past decade, and an award-winning new terminal building was completed in 2008. There are further extensions planned for 2012. The **BMCE** and the **Banque Populaire** have bureaux de change, closed outside office hours, and there are ATMs. Euros may be acceptable to taxi drivers. A *petit taxi* (three passengers) or *grand taxi* (six passengers) from the airport should cost 100-150dh (more after 2000) to the medina or Guéliz, and takes 15 minutes. Although fares are fixed price, published on an airport noticeboard, taxi drivers still try to charge more. Agree the price first. Alternatively, there's a handy airport shuttle bus, No 19, which runs every 30 minutes to Jemaâ el Fna and stops at most hotels in Guéliz, Hivernage and the Palmeraie; 20dh single, 30dh return. For the quickest connection to the train or bus station, your best bet is to take a 15-minute taxi ride and agree the fare. If you're staying in a riad, it's normal practice to arrange a meeting point at the edge of the medina, from where someone will escort you; finding a riad on your own is difficult. You can also ask your riad to arrange airport transfer for about 200dh, which saves a lot of hassle.

From the **railway station** to the heart of the *ville nouvelle* is a 15-minute walk; Jemaâ el Fna and the old city is a further 20-minute walk. A taxi into the city from the station is around 15dh; alternatively, take bus No 3 or 8 from outside the station along Avenue Hassan II and Avenue Mohammed V, to the medina.

Inter-city public **buses** arrive at Bab Doukkala bus station or *gare routière*, a 15-minute walk from Jemaâ el Fna. Bus companies **CTM** and **Supratours** also stop at Bab Doukkala

48 hours in the city

The highlights of the city are less its museums and historic sites than the streets and souks of its medina, and you should allow plenty of time for wandering, stopping for mint tea and getting inevitably lost. **Jemaâ el Fna** makes a good place to start with a fresh orange juice. **Rue Riad Zitoun el Jedid**, to the southeast of the square, is an easily navigated introduction to the medina that takes you down to the impressive riad/palace museums of **Dar Si Said** and **Palais La Bahia**, hopefully before the bus tours arrive. The **Saâdian Tombs** are also a must-do, but can get very crowded. Get some lunch around here before heading north again to the **Koutoubia Mosque** – non-Muslims are not allowed in but the **Jardin de la Koutoubia** is a good spot for a post-prandial wander, and has views of the minaret. Shopping in the souks can be overwhelming – it's a good idea to restrict yourself to perusing on day one, perhaps up Rue Mouassine or Rue Semarine. Then grab a drink on one of the café terraces overlooking Jemaâ el Fna as it comes to life at sundown. If you're feeling brave, you could then descend to eat at one of its stalls, or, for something a little smarter, catch a *petit taxi* to one of the excellent restaurants in the *ville nouvelle*.

On day two, catch the **souks** at their best early in the morning and grab a bargain or two before heading to the **Medersa Ben Youssef**, the city's architectural jewel. **Café des Épices**, or its sibling **Terraces des Épices** make great lunch spots, after which you could head east out to the **tanneries**, or north to **Sidi Bel Abbes**, taking in plenty of street life en route. Catch a taxi to the calming and colourful **Jardin Majorelle** for a wander among the greenery and glimpses of electric blue, before changing into something smart for dinner at one of the medina's atmospheric riad restaurants.

but have their main termini in Guéliz near the train station. ⇥ *See Transport, page 67, for further details.*

Getting around
Marrakech is a spread-out city, built on a plain – hence the large number of mopeds and bicycles; rental of a two-wheeler is an option, though not without risk in the chaotic traffic. Short taxi journeys in Marrakech should not be more than 10 or 15dh – try to have change and insist on using the meter even though you may be told that it is broken. The most picturesque way to drive around is in a calèche, a horse-drawn carriage, but it is perfectly possible to explore the centre on foot.

Hassle The 'hassle' which deterred some visitors in the past is reduced a little thanks to the unseen but ever-vigilant **Brigade Touristique** and the predominant atmosphere is relaxed. If you are robbed or hassled, the Brigade Touristique is based on the Mamounia side of the Koutoubia, near the CMH petrol station (look for the blue and yellow livery), in a small building on a public square with a few trees.

Tourist information **Office du Tourisme** ① *Pl Abd el Moumen Ben Ali (on Av Mohammed V opposite Café Negoçiants), T0524-436131, Mon-Fri 0830-1830*. **Conseil Régional du Tourisme** ① *Pl Youssef Ibn Tachfine, opposite Koutoubia, T0524-385261, Mon-Fri 0830-1830*.

Background

The city

In some early European maps Marrakech appears as 'Morocco city', although 'Maraksh' is the Arabic name. The origins of the name are obscure: some see it as a corruption of 'aghmat-urika', the name of an early town. The city is surrounded by extensive palm groves, into which suburbs are gradually spreading. Yet there are also sandy, arid areas near and, even, within the city which give it a semi-Saharan character.

And then, there are the mountains. Arriving from Fès or Meknès you run alongside the bald arid Jebilet: 'the little mountains', or cross them at Sidi Bou Othmane as you come from Casablanca or Rabat. Perhaps the most beautiful approach to Marrakech is on the N7, from Casablanca and Sidi Bennour, which crosses the Plateau des Gantours and the end of the Jebilet. However, from most points in Marrakech, cloud and heat haze allowing, it is the High Atlas, the Adrar (literally 'the mountains'), which dominate. At times the optical illusion is such that the snow-covered mountain wall appears to rise from just behind the city.

Marrakech is Morocco's fourth largest city. The population is around 1.5 million, although nearer two million including the suburbs. Its people are a mix of Arab and Amazigh; many are recent migrants from surrounding rural regions and further south. For centuries an important regional market place, Marrakech now has a booming service economy and there is still a wide range of handicraft production and small-scale industry, particularly in the medina. Out in the western suburbs are new factories.

Increasingly, tourism is seen as the mainstay of the city's economy. Marrakech is one of the major tourist attractions of Morocco and many of the city's large number of unemployed or under-employed supplement their incomes by casual work with tourists.

Almoravid origins and role

Marrakech was first founded in 1062 by Youssef Ibn Tachfine, the Almoravid leader, as a base from which to control the High Atlas mountains. A kasbah, Dar al Hajar, was built close to the site of the Koutoubia Mosque. Under Youssef Ben Tachfine, Marrakech became the region's first major urban settlement. Within the walls were mosques, palaces and extensive orchards and market gardens, made possible by an elaborate water transfer and irrigation system. The population was probably a mixture of people of black-African descent from the Oued Draâ, Imazighen from the Souss Valley and the nearby Atlas, and Amazigh Jews. The city attracted leading medieval thinkers from outside Marrakech.

Marrakech was taken by the Almohads in 1147, who almost totally destroyed and then rebuilt the city, making it the capital of their extensive empire. Under the Almohad Sultan Abd el Moumen, the Koutoubia Mosque was built on the site of Almoravid buildings, with the minaret added by Ya'qub al Mansour. Under the latter, Marrakech gained palaces, gardens and irrigation works, and again became a centre for musicians, writers and academics, but on his death it declined and fell into disarray.

Merinid neglect and Saâdian revival

While the Merinids added several *medersas* to Marrakech, Fès received much more of their attention and was preferred as the capital, although from 1374 to 1386 Marrakech was the centre of a separate principality. Marrakech was revitalized by the Saâdians from 1524, with the rebuilding of the Ben Youssef Mosque and the construction by Ahmed al Mansour Ad Dahbi of the El Badi Palace and the Saâdian Tombs. Marrakech also became an important trading post, due to its location between the Sahara and the Atlantic.

Alaouite Marrakech

The Alaouites took control of Marrakech in 1668. In the early 18th century the city suffered from Moulay Ismaïl's love of Meknès, with many of the major buildings, notably the El Badi Palace, stripped to glorify the new capital. The destructive effects of this period were compounded by the civil strife following his death. However, from 1873, under Alaouite Sultan Moulay Hassan I and his son, the city's prestige was re-established. A number of the city's fine palaces date from this time and are still open to visitors.

Early 20th century: Glaoui rule

From 1898 until independence, Marrakech was the nerve-centre of southern Morocco, ruled practically as a personal fiefdom by the Glaoui family from the central High Atlas. The French took control of Marrakech and its region in 1912, crushing an insurrection by a claimant to the Sultanate. Their policy in the vast and rugged southern territories was to govern through local rulers, rather as the British worked with the Rajahs of India.

With French support, Pacha T'hami el Glaoui extended his control over all areas of the south. His autonomy from central authority was considerable, his cruelty notorious. And, of course, there were great advantages in this system, in the form of profits from the new French-developed mines. In the 1930s, Marrakech saw the development of a fine *ville nouvelle*, Guéliz, all wide avenues of jacarandas and simple, elegant bungalow houses and, on acquiring a railway line terminus, Marrakech reaffirmed its status as capital of the south. It was at this time, when travel for pleasure was still the preserve of the privileged of Europe, that Marrakech began to acquire its reputation as a retreat for the wealthy.

Capital of the south

In recent decades Marrakech has grown enormously, its population swelled by civil servants and armed forces personnel. Migrants are attracted by the city's reputation as 'city of the poor', where even the least qualified can find work of some kind. For many rural people, the urban struggle is hard and, as the Tachelhit pun puts it, Marrakech is ma-ra-kish, 'the place where they'll eat you if they can'.

North of the medina, new neighbourhoods like Daoudiate and Issil have grown up next to the Université Cadi Ayyad and the mining school. South of the medina, Sidi Youssef Ben Ali, referred to as SYBA, is an extension of the old town and has a reputation for rebellion. West of Guéliz, north of the Essaouira road, are the vast new housing areas of Massira, part low-rise social housing, part villa developments. The most upmarket area is on the Circuit de la Palmeraie. Little by little, the original farmers are being bought out, and desirable homes with lawns and pools behind high walls are taking over from vegetable plots under the palm trees. East of the medina is the vast Amelkis development, a gated community complete with golf course and the discrete Amenjana 'resort'. Here the money and privilege are accommodated in an area equal to one third of the crowded medina.

Future of Marrakech

The early 21st century saw Marrakech in an upbeat mood. The Brigade Touristique, set up to reduce the hassling of tourists, has been reasonably successful. Tourist activity, property development and riad businesses were booming during the first decade of the new millennium, but, with the global economic recession post-2008, this progress has reached a plateau. The ongoing problem for the city is how to deal with the influx of visitors. Certain monuments have reached saturation point: the exquisite Saâdian tombs, for example, are home to a semi-permanent people jam. And, while being packed with people is an important part of the attraction of Jemaâ el Fna, there is the danger that the magic of the place will eventually be diluted by the massive numbers of visitors. The square is now closed to traffic for some of the time, but the roads around the edge of the medina are hellishly busy.

In April 2011 an explosion rocked the famed Café Argana in the main square of Jemaâ el Fna. Though the **Café Argana** is being rebuilt at time of writing, and after a short hiatus where travellers avoided Marrakech, the city has fully recovered.

The 'Venice of Morocco'?

Marrakech continues to draw the visitors in and to maintain its hold on the Western imagination. The setting is undeniably exotic, eccentricities are tolerated and (rather less honourably) domestic help is cheap. Features in international decoration magazines fuel the demand for property; major monuments are being restored. One-time resident the late Yves St Laurent even dubbed Marrakech 'the Venice of Morocco' – which might seem an appropriate description on a February day with torrential rain on Jemaâ el Fna.

Still, the Red City retains a sense of rawness, despite the creeping gentrification, and remains the closest Orient one can find within a few hours, flight of the grey north European winter. Provided city authorities can keep vehicle pollution in check, it looks set to maintain its popularity.

Places in Marrakech → *For listings, see pages 45-68.*

Central Marrakech is clearly divided into two parts: the large historic city, the **medina**, and the *ville nouvelle*, **Guéliz**. The focal point of the medina, and indeed of the whole city, is the **Jemaâ el Fna**, an open place full of street entertainers and food sellers, adjacent to which are the most important souks. Handily for the tourist, it is located in the middle of the main areas of historic sights. North of Jemaâ el Fna are the **souks** and the **Sidi Ben Youssef Mosque**, the city's main mosque after the Koutoubia. On a walk in this neighbourhood, you can visit the **Almoravid Koubba**, the **Medersa Ben Youssef**, and the **Museum of Marrakech**. South of Jemaâ el Fna, down Riad Zitoun el Kedim, is an area of **palaces**, the **Saâdian Tombs** and a small ethnographic museum, the **Maison Tiskiwine**.

If you are staying in a riad, you may well be in the **Bab Doukkala** or **Leksour/ Mouassine** neighbourhoods, the former on the Guéliz side of the medina. The latter is very central, just north of Jemaâ el Fna, and is one of the most chic enclaves, home to bijou gallery places like the **Dar Cherifa** *café littéraire*. Bab Doukkala is handier for the bus station. For visitors with more time, the Thursday flea market at **Bab el Khemis** is ideal for those seeking gems amongst junk and second-hand treasures. Another point of interest are the **tanneries** at Bab Debbagh.

A popular feature of a visit to Marrakech is a tour of the gardens. This will include the **Jardin Majorelle**, quite close to Bab Doukkala, the **Menara**, a large square pool set in a vast olive grove south of Guéliz, and the **Agdal**, another olive grove close to the Sidi Youssef Ben Ali neighbourhood. To the east and north of Marrakech, across the Oued Issil, is the **Palmeraie**. Close to the Medina, the gardens between Koutoubia and Mamounia have been totally replanted with roses. Even once scruffy Arset Moulay Slimane, opposite the Municipality on your way to Jemaâ el Fna, has been spruced up.

Most visitors will spend some time in Guéliz, the suburb laid out by the French in the 1920s. Despite all the new apartment buildings and traffic, it is worth a wander for its cafés,

Jemaâ el Juice

Ask people about their impressions of Jemaâ el Fna and they'll mention the snake charmers, the food, the acrobats, the swarming mass of humanity, but also the orange juice. Around the edges of the square, from dawn to dusk and beyond, are stalls piled high with immaculately stacked oranges; a 4dh glass of refreshing juice from the army of drink vendors is an important part of the Jemaâ el Fna experience. Depending on which stall you get it from, it may come slightly watered down with squash, and the locals complain when there's no sugar added, but it's invariably delicious and absurdly cheap. Expect to pay 10dh if it's freshly squeezed (and therefore entirely unadulterated) in front of you, or for grapefruit.

upmarket boutiques and art galleries, and it has many of the city's best restaurants. The main thoroughfare is Avenue Mohammed V and the evening promenade here is popular.

Jemaâ el Fna

The Jemaâ el Fna, unique in Morocco, is both the greatest pull for tourists and still a genuine social area for Marrakchi and those flooding in from the surrounding regions. 'La Place' is full of people hawking their goods or talents and others watching, walking, talking and arguing. It is particularly memorable during Ramadan when the day's fast ends. Whatever the time of day or year, Jemaâ el Fna is somewhere that visitors return to again and again, responding to the magnetic pull that affects locals as much as tourists, to mingle with the crowd or watch from the terrace of the **Café de France** or **Les Terrasses de L'Alhambra**.

Background

Jemaâ el Fna means 'assembly of the dead' and may refer to the traditional display of the heads of criminals executed here until the 19th century. In 1956, the government attempted to close down the square by converting it into a corn market and car park, but it soon reverted to its traditional role. In the late 1980s, the bus station was moved out to Bab Doukkala. In 1994, the square was fully tarmacked for the GATT meeting. The food stands were reorganized and the orange juice sellers issued with smart red fezzes and white gloves. Pickpockets are occasionally a problem on Jemaâ el Fna, and visitors should beware when standing in crowds around the buskers. Keep plenty of small change handy for the various entertainments and orange juice, and keep wallets or handbags out of view.

At 'La Place'

During the day you can explore the stalls and collections of goods: fruit, herbs and spices, clothes, shoes, alarm clocks and radios, as well as handicrafts. There are snake charmers and monkey tamers, watersellers and wildly grinning Gnaoua musicians with giant metal castanets, all too ready to pose for photographs. Sheltering from the sun under their umbrellas, the fortune tellers and public scribes await their clients. In the evening, the crowd changes again, a mix of students and people pausing on the way home from work, smart tourists strolling to restaurants in the medina – and backpackers ready for hot tagine or harira soup at one of the foodstalls. You may see Ouled el Moussa tumblers or a storyteller enthralling the crowd. Sometimes there are boxers, and usually there are groups of musicians: after much effort to extract a few dirhams from the crowd, an

◻1 Marrakech

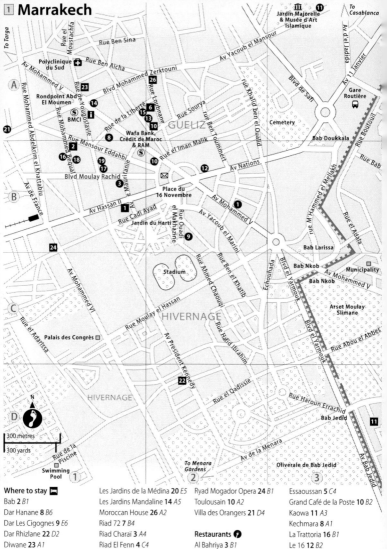

Where to stay 🛏

Bab 2 *B1*
Dar Hanane 8 *B6*
Dar Les Cigognes 9 *E6*
Dar Rhizlane 22 *D2*
Diwane 23 *A1*
du Pacha 6 *A2*
Fashion 1 *B1*
La Maison Arabe 18 *B4*
La Mamounia 11 *D3*
La Sultana 19 *E5*
Le Nid 16 *D5*

Les Jardins de la Médina 20 *E5*
Les Jardins Mandaline 14 *A5*
Moroccan House 26 *A2*
Riad 72 7 *B4*
Riad Charaï 3 *A4*
Riad El Fenn 4 *C4*
Riad el Ouarda 5 *A5*
Riad Kaiss 17 *D5*
Riad Malika 12 *B4*
Riad Marianis 15 *B5*
Riad Tizwa 13 *B4*
Riad Tlaatawa-Sitteen 25 *B5*

Ryad Mogador Opera 24 *B1*
Toulousain 10 *A2*
Villa des Orangers 21 *D4*

Restaurants 🍴

Al Bahriya 3 *B1*
Al Fassia 1 *B2*
Bistro Thai 9 *B2*
Café du Livre 13 *A2*
Café Les Négociants 14 *A1*
Catanzaro 15 *A1*
Dar Zellij 2 *A4*

Essaoussan 5 *C4*
Grand Café de la Poste 10 *B2*
Kaowa 11 *A3*
Kechmara 8 *A1*
La Trattoria 16 *B1*
Le 16 12 *B2*
Le Bagatelle 17 *B1*
Le Carioca 18 *B1*
Le Foundouk 4 *B5*
Nid'Cigogne 6 *E5*
Rotisserie de la Paix 19 *B1*
Vlème Ave 21 *A1*

To Fès & The Palmeraie

To Souk el Khemis

Zaouia of
Sidi Bel Abbes
3

Bab el Khemis

Bab
Taghzaoute
5

SIDI BEL ABBES

2

Zaouia of Sidi
Ben Slimane el Jazouli

Rue el Gza

**RIAD
LAAROUSS**

Rue Bab Tagzaoute

Rue Assouel

Rue Bab Bab el Khemis

Route des Remparts

**EL
MOUKEF**

Cemetery

Bab Debbagh

Tannery

To Amelkis

RIAD EL AROOS

Rue Riad Laarouss

25
15

13
2

Rue Bab
Doukkala

Dar el Bacha

Ben Youssef
Mosque

Medersa
Ben Youssef

Rue de Bab Debbagh

4

Doukkala

Bab Doukkala
Mosque
7
12
18

Av Dar el Ghaoui

Almoravid
Koubba

Musée de
Marrakech

Rue Issebbrjye

8

MOUASSINE

SOUKS

Rue de Bab Allen

To Amelkis

Rue Sidi el Yamani

Souk Semmarine

LEKSOUR

Bab Ksour
4
5

Rue Fatima Zohra

Derb Dabachi

Rue Sidi Boulabada

**Jemaâ el
Fna**

Rue Kennaria

Rue Douar Graoua

Rue du Djenan

Koutoubia
Esplanade

Rue Bab Agnaou

Rue Riad Zitoun el Kedim

Rue Riad Zitoun el Jedid

Dar Si Said

**Koutoubia
Mosque**

Av Houmane el Fetouaki

Brigade
Touristique
Pol

Av Homman el Fetouaki

Maison
Tiskiwine

**Bahia
Palace**

Cemetery

21

Rue Sidi Mimoun

17

Place des
Ferblantiers
16

ben Chegra

Bab
Agnaou

Bab
Berima

MELLAH

Mosque de
la Kasbah

El Badi
Palace

9

Bab Rob

Saadian
Tombs
6 **19**

Rue de la Kasbah

BERR IMA

Cemetery

**Royal Palace
(Dar el Makhzen)**

To Airport

E

4

To Oukaïmeden

KASBAH

5

20

6

Agdal Gardens

acoustic band will get some Berbers dancing, while around a hissing gas lamp a group will perform a song by Jil Jilala, an activist group popular in the 1970s.

More recent attractions include the *nakkachat*, women with syringes full of henna, ready to pipe a design onto your hands. 'Hook the ring over the coke bottle' is popular, or you can try bowling a football between two impossibly narrow goal posts for a dirham or two. You may find an astrologist-soothsayer tracing out his diagram of the future on the tarmac with a stubby piece of chalk. A modern variation on the traditional *halka* or storyteller's circle touches harsh social reality: local people listen to a true tale told with dignity by the relatives of a victim of poverty or injustice. And should you need an aphrodisiac, there are stalls with tea urns selling cinnamon and ginseng tea and little dishes of black, powdery *slilou*, a spicey sweet paste.

Thanks to campaigning by a team led by Spanish writer and Marrakech resident Juan Goytisolo, Jemaâ el Fna has received UNESCO recognition for its place in humankind's oral tradition.

Koutoubia Mosque

The 65-m high minaret of the Koutoubia Mosque dominates the whole of Marrakech. Visible from afar, it provided the focal point for urban planner Henri Prost when he laid out the modern neighbourhood of Guéliz. The Koutoubia is clearly visible as, unlike the Qarawiyin Mosque in Fès, it is set apart from the dense building of the old town. An unlikely legend goes that as this structure overlooked the harem, only a blind muezzin was allowed to climb it to call the faithful to prayer. The name 'Koutoubia' derives from the Arabic *kutub* (books) and means the 'Booksellers' Mosque', reflecting the fact that the trade of selling manuscripts was conducted in a souk close to the mosque. As this is a place of prayer, and in every way the most important mosque in the city, dress decently if you are going to approach the site to view it at length. Behind the mosque are gardens and some good photo opportunities.

Background
Unusually, the Koutoubia is a double mosque, both parts dating from the reign of the second Almohad ruler, Abd el Mumin (1130-1163). Standing on the esplanade facing the minaret, the ruins of the first Koutoubia are behind railings to your right (first excavated in the late 1940s, and re-explored recently). The bases of the prayer hall's columns, and the cisterns under the courtyard are clearly visible. The ground plan of the second Koutoubia, still standing, is the same as that of the ruined one (17 naves). The Almohad mosque at Tin Mal (see page 86), open for visits by non-Muslims, has a similar plan.

The site of the mosque is itself historic and was originally occupied by a late 11th-century kasbah, the Almoravid Dar al Hajar. The successful Almohads destroyed much of the Almoravid city and, in 1147, built a large mosque, close to the fortress. In all likelihood they had to do this because, puritan as they were and considering the Almoravids to be heretics, they could not pray in a tainted building. Unfortunately, the orientation of the new Almohad mosque was not quite right – the focus point in a mosque is the direction of Mecca and should be indicated by the mihrab, or prayer niche. The solution was to build a second mosque – the present Koutoubia – even though the faithful at prayer can correct this directional problem themselves, under the direction of the imam, once the right direction has been worked out.

Thus two mosques existed for some time side by side, the first probably functioning as a sort of annexe. Given Almohad religious fervour, the congregations were no doubt large.

Kids in Marrakech

There's plenty to entertain children in Marrakech, from the Jemaâ el Fna snake charmers to acrobats that will come somersaulting your way the moment you sit outside at a restaurant. But there's little that's specifically designed for kids. A day out at a pool outside the city (see box, page 66) is a good bet, and a trip to the mountains provides some needed space. A horse-drawn calèche tour of the city walls is a good way to see something without the scrum of street level, and places such as the Menara gardens sometimes have camels that can be ridden through the palm groves. For real wide-eyed excitement go for an early morning balloon ride over the nearby countryside (page 65).

Today, the bricked-up spaces on the northwest wall of the Koutoubia Mosque indicate the doors which connected them. However, the older structure fell into disrepair and eventual ruin. The excavations of 1948 also revealed a *maqsura*, or screen, in front of the mihrab, which could be wound up through the floor to protect the Sultan, and a *minbar*, or pulpit, which was moved into position on wooden rollers. The two cisterns in the centre may have been from a previous Almoravid structure. On the eastern flank of this mosque was an arcade of which a niche and the remains of one arch remain.

Existing Koutoubia Mosque

The existing Koutoubia Mosque was built by Abd el Mumin in 1162. The minaret is 12.5 m wide and 67.5 m to the tip of the cupola on the lantern, and is the mosque's principal feature, rightly ranked alongside later Almohad structures, the Hassan Tower in Rabat and the Giralda in Seville. The minaret, composed of six rooms, one on top of the other, was a great feat of engineering in its day and influenced several subsequent buildings in Morocco. The cupola on top is a symmetrical square structure topped by a ribbed dome and three golden orbs, which are alleged to have been made from the melted-down jewellery of successive Almohad leader, Yaqoub al Mansour's wife, in penance for her having eaten three grapes during the Ramadan fast. The cupola has two windows on each side, above which is a stone panel in the *darj w ktaf*, 'step-and-shoulder', motif. (For a close-up view of the top of the mosque and this design feature, consult a 100dh banknote.) The main tower has a band of coloured tiles at the top.

The Koutoubia, a vast structure for 12th-century North Africa, had to be a mosque equal to the ambitions of the Western Caliphate. It is held to be the high point of Almohad building, a cathedral-mosque of classic simplicity. It is here that the innovations of Hispano-Moorish art – stalactite cupolas, painted wooden ceilings – reach perfection. There are perspectives of horseshoe arches, no doubt an aid to contemplation. Although the prayer hall is off-limits to non-Muslim visitors, an idea of what it is like can be gained at the Tin Mal mosque in the High Atlas (see page 86). The unique *minbar* (preacher's chair), set against this apparent simplicity, is all decoration and variety, and very much in keeping with the elaborate taste of Ummayad Spain. (The original *minbar*, also recently restored, can be viewed at the Badi Palace.) Both prayer hall and chair were to be a source of inspiration for later generations of builders and decorators.

Ultimately, the Koutoubia is striking because it is the work of one ruler, Abd el Mumin. Comparable buildings in western Islam – the Great Mosque of Córdoba and the Alhambra – were built over a couple of centuries.

North of Jemaâ el Fna: souks and monuments

Many of the **souks** of Marrakech retain their original function and a morning's souking is one of the great pleasures of the city. Before leaping into impulse purchases, get an idea of prices in shops in Guéliz, or in the **Ensemble Artisanal** on Mohammed V. Once you have threaded your way up Souk Semmarine, onto Souk el Kebir and past Souk Cherratine, you are in the neighbourhood of some of the city's most important Islamic monuments, the **Almoravid Koubba** and **Medersa Ben Youssef**. (Note that there is a rather bureaucratic enforcement of the order in which you see the three Islamic monuments – Museum, Medersa and Koubba – and the Koubba must be the last of the three.) The **Museum of Marrakech** and the **Fondation Dar Belarj Museum** are also evidence of private money creating new heritage sites.

Souks

The main souks lie to the north of Jemaâ el Fna. The entrance to them is to the left of the mosque. Follow this round to the left and then turn right into the main thoroughfare, **Souk Semmarine**. Alternatively, enter through the small tourist market, further round to the left on Jemaâ el Fna. Souk Semmarine is a busy place, originally the textiles market, and, although there are a number of large, expensive tourist shops, there are still some cloth sellers. To the left is a *kissaria* (small covered alley) selling clothes. The first turning on the right leads past **Souk Larzal**, a wool market, and **Souk Btana**, a sheepskin market, to **Rahba Kedima**, the old corn market, now selling a range of goods, including traditional cures and cosmetics, spices, vegetables and cheap jewellery, and with some good carpet shops. Walk back onto the main souk via a short alley with wood-carved goods. Here the souk forks into **Souk el Attarine** (perfumers' souk) on the left and **Souk el Kebir** on the right.

To the right of Souk el Kebir is the **Criée Berbère**, where carpets and jallabahs are sold. This was where slaves, mainly from across the Sahara, were auctioned until 1912. Further on is the **Souk des Bijoutiers**, with jewellery. To the left (west) of Souk el Kebir is a network of *kissarias*, selling western goods. Beyond this is the **Souk Cherratine**, with leather goods, somewhere to bargain for camel or cowhide bags, purses and belts.

Continuing back on the other side of the *kissarias* is the **Souk des Babouches**, a far better place to buy slippers than in the tourist shops. This feeds into Souk el Attarine, the spice and perfume souk, which itself leads back into Souk Semmarine. West of the Souk el Attarine is the carpenters' **Souk Chouari**. From here, walk on to see a Saâdian fountain and the 16th-century **Mouassine Mosque**. South of Souk Chouari is the **Souk des Teinturiers**, or dyers' market, where wool recently dyed is festooned over the walkways. Nearby are the blacksmiths' and coppersmiths' souks.

Musée de Marrakech

ⓘ *Pl Ben Youssef, T0524-441893, www.museedemarrakech.ma, daily 0900-1800, 40dh, 60dh with the Medersa Ben Youssef and Koubba. After the entrance courtyard (good café on left, bookshop on right).*

The entrance to the museum is just off the open area in front of the Almoravid Koubba and it is housed in Dar M'nebhi, the early 20th-century palace of a former Moroccan minister of war. The simple whitewashed walls of the domestic wing shelter temporary exhibitions of generally unimpressive contemporary art. Off the main courtyard, protected by a plexi-glass roof and a brass chandelier the size of a small UFO, are displays of Koran manuscripts, coins, ceramics and textiles. Note the Portuguese influence in the elaborate wooden façades to the rooms on the left. A small passageway to the left of the main reception room takes you

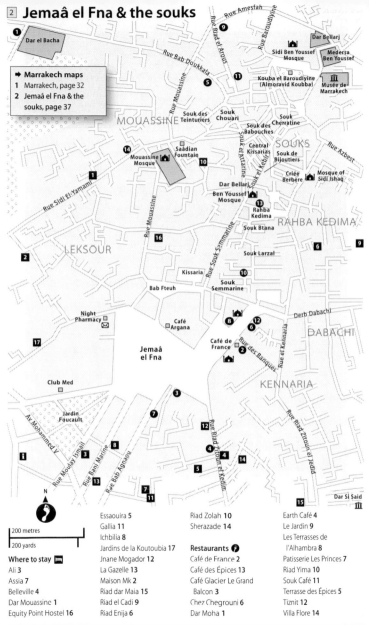

➡ **Marrakech maps**
1 Marrakech, page 32
2 Jemaâ el Fna & the
   souks, page 37

Dar el Bacha

Rue Amesfah

Rue Bab Doukkala

Rue Riad el Arous

Rue Baroudiyine

Dar Bellarj

Sidi Ben Youssef
Mosque

Medersa
Ben Youssef

Kouba el Baroudiyine
(Almoravid Koubba)

Musée de
Marrakech

MOUASSINE

Rue Mouassine

Souk des
Teinturiers

Souk
Chouari

Souk
Cherratine

Souk des
Babouches

Souk el Attarine

Souk el Kebir

Central
Kissarias

Souk de
Bijoutiers

Rue Azbest

Criée
Berbère

Mosque of
Sidi Ishaq

Saâdian
Fountain

Mouassine
Mosque

Dar Bellarj

Ben Youssef
Mosque

Rahba
Kedima

RAHBA KEDIMA

LEKSOUR

Rue Sidi El-Yamami

Rue Mouassine

Souk Btana

Souk Larzal

Rue Souk Semmarine

Kissaria

Souk
Semmarine

Bab Fteuh

Night
Pharmacy

Café
Argana

Jemaâ
el Fna

Café de
France

Rue des Banques

Derb Dabachi

DABACHI

Rue el Kennaria

KENNARIA

Club Med

Jardin
Foucault

Av. Mohammed V

Rue Moulay Ismail

Rue Bani Marine

Rue Bab Agnaou

Rue Riad Zitoun el Kedim

Rue Riad Zitoun el Jedid

Dar Si Said

N

200 metres
200 yards

Where to stay 🛏
Ali 3
Assia 7
Belleville 4
Dar Mouassine 1
Equity Point Hostel 16

Essaouira 5
Gallia 11
Ichbilia 8
Jardins de la Koutoubia 17
Jnane Mogador 12
La Gazelle 13
Maison Mk 2
Riad dar Maia 15
Riad el Cadi 9
Riad Enija 6

Riad Zolah 10
Sherazade 14

Restaurants 🍴
Café de France 2
Café des Épices 13
Café Glacier Le Grand
   Balcon 3
Chez Chegrouni 6
Dar Moha 1

Earth Café 4
Le Jardin 9
Les Terrasses de
   l'Alhambra 8
Patisserie Les Princes 7
Riad Yima 10
Souk Café 11
Terrasse des Épices 5
Tiznit 12
Villa Flore 14

through to the restored hammam, now home to a small collection of early engravings on Morocco. The museum as a whole is worth a visit more for the building than the exhibits.

Medersa Ben Youssef
ⓘ *Daily 0900-1800, 40dh or 60dh with the Museum and Koubba.*

Standing with the Almoravid Koubba behind you, the minaret of the large 12th-century Ben Youssef Mosque, rebuilt in the 19th century, is clearly visible. Turning right out of the Musée de Marrakech, follow the street round to the entrance to the city's most important Islamic monument, the 16th-century Medersa Ben Youssef. One of the few Islamic buildings open to the general public, it has been restored by the Fondation Ben Jelloun and is now Marrakech's architectural highlight. Cool, calm corridors, beautiful arches, *zellige* tiles and the light reflecting in the central pool make it a breathtaking place to visit. Founded in 1564-1565 by the Saâdian Sultan Moulay Abdellah, on the site of a previous Merinid *medersa*, it functioned as a boarding school for students of the religious sciences and law. The Medersa is centred around a square courtyard containing a rectangular pool, and with arcades on two sides. Each student had a separate cell with a sleeping loft and a window looking onto the courtyard. Note the much worn but still fine cedar wood of the upper façades around the courtyard. You will see fine *zellige* tiling on the arcade floor, walls and pillars. Inscriptions are in Kufic and cursive lettering, interwoven with floral patterns.

At the far end is the prayer hall covered with an eight-sided wooden dome. Beneath the dome-plaster open-work windows illuminate the tilework. In the *qibla* wall is a five-sided mihrab. Note the stalactite ceiling of the mihrab, and the carved stucco walls with pine cone motif. The inscription here, dedicated to the Sultan, translates as: "I was constructed as a place of learning and prayer by the Prince of the Faithful, the descendant of the seal of the prophets, Abdellah, the most glorious of all Caliphs. Pray for him, all who enter here, so that his greatest hopes may be realized." Note also the massive Carrara marble columns.

On the way out of the Medersa, the toilets on the right of the vestibule have an elaborate stalactite design on the ceiling.

Koubba el Baroudiyine
ⓘ *Pl Ben Youssef, daily 0900-1800, 60dh combined with the Medersa and Museum.*

Now protected by neo-Versailles wrought-iron railings, the 11th-century Almoravid Koubba (Koubba el Baroudiyine) is the only complete Almoravid building surviving in the city. It dates from the reign of Ali bin Youssef (1107-1143) and, perhaps, formed part of the toilet and ablutions facilities of the mosque that at the time existed nearby. At first glance it is a simple building, with a dome surmounting a square stone and brick structure. However, the dome has a design of interlocking arches, plus a star and chevron motif on top. The arches leading into the *koubba* are different on each side. Climb down the stairs to view the ceiling of the dome, noting the range of Almoravid motifs, including the palmette, pine cone and acanthus. Around the corniche is a dedicatory inscription in cursive script. Set into the floor is a small, almost square basin.

Dar Bellarj and around
ⓘ *9 Toulalat Zaouïat Lahdar, T0524-444555, daily 0900-1800, free.*

Turning right out of the Medersa, then left under a covered street, you will come to the entrance of Dar Bellarj, 'the House of Storks', on your left. The building, restored recently by a couple of Swiss artists, dates from the 1930s. Prior to this there was a fondouk on the site which housed the only hospital for birds in North Africa. Here there dwelt a wise man with the gift of curing wounded storks. Today, the building, austerely but simply refurbished, is used primarily as gallery space for contemporary arts.

Just yards from the Medersa Ben Youssef is **Maison de la Photographie** ⓘ *46 Rue Ahal Fès, T0524-385721, www.maisondelaphotographie.com, daily 0930-1900, 40dh, children free*, a recently opened gallery of vintage Moroccan photographs. Thousands of sepia-tinted photos and glass negatives dating to the mid-1800s are displayed over the three floors in a restored riad, with a café on the roof terrace; this is well worth a visit.

North of Medersa Ben Youssef

North of the Medersa Ben Youssef, you can wander through more recent residential neighbourhoods, built on the site of former orchards and market gardens. Whereas Fès has steep and narrow streets, accessible only by pedestrians and mules, flat Marrakech is teeming with bicycles and mopeds, mini-taxis and handcarts. Eventually, your wandering might take you to the open square of Bab Taghzaoute and on to **Zaouïa of Sidi Bel Abbes**. Usually considered the most important of the seven saints of Marrakech, Bel Abbes was born in Ceuta in 1130. He championed the cause of the blind in Marrakech and was patronized by Sultan Yaqoub al Mansour. You are free to wander through the religious complex, though non-Muslims are barred from the mausoleum. It's a striking place, with bright squares and shady alleyways. A series of arches is filled with potted plants and blind people chatting and waiting to receive alms. Nearby is the **Zaouïa of Sidi Ben Slimane el Jazouli**, a 14th-century sufi.

Kasbah quarter

Bab Agnaou, meaning the 'gate of the black people', marks the entrance to the kasbah quarter. To get to it, follow Avenue Prince Moulay Rachid (also known as Rue Bab Agnaou) south from Jemaâ el Fna, or enter the medina at Bab Rob. The kasbah quarter dates from the late 12th century and the reign of the Almohad Sultan Ya'qub al Mansour. Bab Agnaou is also Almohad. The gateway itself is surrounded by a series of arches within a rectangle of floral designs, with a shell or palmette in each corner and an outer band of Kufic inscription.

The road from the gate leads to Rue de la Kasbah, turn right along here and then take the first left. On this road is the much restored **Kasbah Mosque**, dating from 1190. The minaret has Almohad *darj w ktaf* and *shabka* (net) motifs on alternate sides, with a background of green tiles, above which is a band of coloured tiles. Though not as impressive as the tower of the Koutoubia Mosque, the minaret is a notable landmark en route to the Saâdian Tombs. The entrance to these lies directly to the right of the mosque.

Saâdian Tombs

ⓘ *Rue de la Kasbah, daily 0900-1645, 10dh. Try to visit early in the day as the place gets very crowded with tour groups.*

The late 16th-century Saâdian Tombs were discovered thanks to aerial photography in 1917, having been sealed off by Moulay Ismaïl in the 17th century in a vain attempt to condemn the Saâdian rulers to oblivion. A series of chambers around a small garden, decorated with carved cedar and plaster, is the final and, ultimately rather moving, resting place of the Saâdian family. The mihrab of the first main burial chamber is particularly impressive. Here lies the prince Moulay Yazid. The second room contains the tomb of Ahmed al Mansour. The second and older mausoleum was built for the tombs of Ahmed al Mansour's mother, Lalla Messaouda, and Mohammed esh Sheikh, founder of the Saâdians. In the rather dilapidated garden and courtyard are the tombs of numerous other princelings and followers.

El Badi Palace

ⓘ *0900-1645, 10dh plus another 10dh to see the Koutoubia minbar.*

The huge barren spaces of the ruined 16th-century El Badi Palace come as a bit of a shock after the cramped streets of the Marrakech medina. Orange trees grow in what were once enormous pools in the central courtyard, and storks nest noisily on the ruined walls. For five days in July, El Badi comes alive for the annual **Popular Arts Festival** (see page 62), most of the year, however, it is a quiet sort of place, the high thick walls protecting the vast courtyard from the noise of the surrounding streets.

To get there from the Bab Agnaou, head right inside ramparts, and then take the second right. The road leads more or less directly to Place des Ferblantiers, a square with a number of workshops where they make lanterns and items in tin. Pass through Bab Berima, the gate on the southern side. The entrance to the palace is on the right, between high *pisé* walls.

The palace was built by the Saâdian Sultan Ahmed al Mansour ed-Dahbi (the Golden) between 1578 and 1593, following his accession after his victory over the Portuguese at the Battle of the Three Kings, at Ksar el Kebir in northern Morocco. It marks the height of Saâdian power, the centrepiece of an imperial capital. It was a lavish display of the best craftsmanship of the period, using the most expensive materials, including gold, marble and onyx. The colonnades were of marble, apparently exchanged with Italian merchants for their equivalent weight in sugar.

The palace was largely destroyed in the 17th century by Moulay Ismaïl, who stripped it of its decorations and fittings and carried them off to Meknès. No austere royal fortress, the Badi was probably a palace for audiences – and it was at one of these great court ceremonies that the building's fate was predicted: 'What do you think of this palace?' asked the Sultan El Mansour. 'When it is demolished, it will make a big pile of earth,' replied a visionary. El Mansour is said to have felt a sinister omen.

The ruins on either side of the courtyard were probably summer houses, the one at the far end being called the **Koubba el Khamsiniya** (The Fifty Pavillion) after either the 50 cubits of its area, or the fact that it once had 50 columns.

The complex contains a small **museum** whose exhibits include the restored *minbar* (the sacred staired Islamic equivalent of a pulpit, from which the Imam delivers sermons) from the Koutoubia Mosque. Mark Minor, one of the conservators from the Metropolitan Museum of Art in New York who carried out the restoration, called it "one of the finest works of art in wood created by mankind." Constructed in Córdoba in Spain in 1139, it is covered in around 100 carvings. The *minbar* remained in use until 1962. The scattered ruins of the palace, with odd fragments of decoration amidst the debris, include also stables and dungeons.

Royal Palace

ⓘ *Not open to the public.*

To the south of the El Badi Palace is the Dar el Makhzen, the modern-day Royal Palace, one of the late King Hassan II's favourite residences. The present king has had a new palace constructed, close to the Mamounia.

Down Riad Zitoun el Jedid: craft museums and palaces

Two museums devoted to Moroccan artistry, both in spectacular settings, sit close together at the south end of Riad Zitoun el Jedid. From Jemaâ el Fna, follow Rue des Banques from just past **Café de France**. At the first junction, follow through to the right onto Riad Zitoun el Jedid. Eventually, on Riad Zitoun el Jedid, you'll see signs indicating the Dar Si Said off to the left and the smaller Maison Tiskiwine.

Dar Si Said

ⓘ *Derb el Bahia, Riad Zitoun el Jedid, T0524-389564, daily 0900-1630, closed Tue, 10dh.*
Built by Si Said, Visir under Moulay el Hassan and half-brother of Ba Ahmed Ben Moussa, Dar Si Said is a late 19th-century palace housing the Museum of Moroccan Arts and Crafts. The collection includes pottery, jewellery, leatherwork and Chichaoua carpets and is particularly strong on Amazigh artefacts. On the first floor is a salon with Hispano-Moorish decoration and cedarwood furniture, while around the garden courtyard you'll find old window and door frames. Look out for a primitive four-seater wooden ferris wheel of the type still found in *moussems* (country fairs) in Morocco. Those interested in traditional Moroccan artefacts will want to continue to the neighbouring Maison Tiskiwin.

Maison Tiskiwin

ⓘ *8 Rue de la Bahia, T0524-389192, www.tiskiwin.com, daily 0930-1230 and 1430-1800, 20dh, children 10dh.*
Between the Dar Si Said and the Bahia Palace a few streets further south is the fantastic Maison Tiskiwin ('the House of the Horns'), home to a fine collection of items related to Northern African and Saharan culture and society. This small museum was lovingly put together by the Dutch art historian Bert Flint, who still lives here, though he has given the museum to Marrakech University. Flint still spends some of the year travelling and collecting to add to the collection, and there is a strong sense of enthusiasm for the artefacts here (in contrast to some of the state-run museums). There are crafts from the Rif and the High Atlas, though the collection focuses primarily on the Sahara, and includes jewellery and costumes, musical instruments, carpets and furniture. The building itself, around a courtyard, is an authentic and well-maintained example of a traditional riad. There are excellent and copious notes in English. Groups tend to visit in the morning – if you go along in the afternoon you may get the museum all to yourself.

Bahia Palace

ⓘ *0900-1700, 10dh.*
Further to the south is the Bahia Palace (Bahia means 'brilliant', and it is). It was built in the last years of the 19th century by the Vizir Ba Ahmed Ben Moussa, or Bou Ahmed, a former slave who exercised power under sultans Moulay Hassan and Abd el Aziz. Sunlight shines through wrought-iron bars creating beautiful patterns on the *zellige* tiles and, in the courtyard, water ripples over green tiles around a beautiful fountain, surrounded by trees. There are tour groups, but there are also plenty of quiet corners in which lingering until they've passed is a pleasure. The palace is a maze of patios planted with fruit trees, passageways and empty chambers with painted ceilings. Guides will tell you that each wife and concubine had a room looking onto the patio. The story goes that Bou Ahmed was so hated that, on his death in 1900, his palace was looted and his possessions stolen by slaves, servants and members of his harem. Subsequently, the building was occupied by the French authorities. Bareness is still a feature of the palace, but it is one that accentuates the beauty of the architecture.

The Jewish quarter

South of the Bahia and east of the El Badi Palace, the *mellah* or Jewish neighbourhood was created in 1558. The Jewish community has all but vanished, and there is little to tell you of its former role in the life of Marrakech. There were several synagogues and, under the control of the rabbis, the area had considerable autonomy. It is worth asking around to be let into one of the synagogues.

Tanneries near Bab Debbagh

The tanneries near Bab Debbagh ('Tanners' Gate') are one of the most interesting (if smelly) sites in Marrakech. Wandering towards the tanners' area, you will in all likelihood be approached by some lad who will offer to show you the tanneries (20dh is a reasonable tip). You will be given a sprig of mint to hold to your nostrils and, through a small metal door, you will be shown an area of foul-smelling pits, where men tread and rinse skins in nauseous liquids and dyes. In small lean-to buildings, you will find other artisans scraping and stretching the skins. Located close to the seasonal Oued Issil, the tanners were on the edge of the city with plenty of water and space to expand away from residential areas.

You will probably be told that there are two tanneries: one Arab, the other Berber. In fact there are several, and workforces are ethnically mixed. There do remain specialities, however, with one set of tanners working mainly on the more difficult cow and camel skins, and the others on goat and sheep skins. Tanning in Marrakech is still a pre-industrial process, alive and functioning not far from the heart of the medina – even though the traditional dyes have largely been replaced with chemical products. See also box, opposite.

Ramparts and gates

The extensive ramparts of Marrakech (20 gates and 200 towers stretching for 16 km) are predominantly Almoravid, excepting those around the Agdal Gardens, although they have been extensively restored since. Reconstruction is a continual process as the *pisé*-cement walls, made of the distinctive earth of the Haouz plains, gradually crumble. The ramparts and gates are one of the distinctive sights of Morocco. A ride in a horse-drawn calèche will allow you to see part of the ramparts. In places, there has been much beautification, with fancy wrought-iron railings and rose gardens taking the place of the dust on the Hivernage side of town.

Bab Rob, near the buses and *grands taxis* on the southwest side of the medina, is Almohad, and is named after the grape juice which could only be brought through this gate. **Bab Debbagh**, on the east side, is an intricate defensive gate with a twisted entrance route and wooden gates, which could shut off the various parts of the building for security. **Bab el Khemis**, on the northeast side, opens into the Souk el Khemis (Thursday market) and an important area of mechanics and craftsmen. Check out the junk-market here on a Sunday morning. There is a small saint's tomb inside the gate building. Bab Doukkala, on the northwest side by the bus station, is a large gate with a horseshoe arch and two towers. The medina side has a horseshoe arch and a cusped, blind arch, with a variation on the *darj w ktaf* (step and shoulder) motif along the top. There are occasional exhibitions in the guardroom inside the gate. The esplanade here has been badly neglected and many of the orange trees have died off. A new road across the palm grove north of **Bab Doukkala** completes the circuit of the ramparts.

Tanning secrets

The tanners are said to have been the first to settle in Marrakech at its foundation, and a gate is named after them, the only one to be named for a craft corporation. 'Bab Debbagh, bab deheb' – 'Tanners' Gate, gold gate' – the old adage goes, in reference to the tanners' prosperity. One legend runs that seven virgins are buried in the foundations of the gate (sisters of the seven protector saints of Marrakech) and that women who desire a child should offer them candles and henna. Another legend says that Bab Debbagh is inhabited by Malik Gharub, a genie who dared to lead a revolt against Sidna Suleyman, the Black King, only to be condemned to tan a cowhide and cut out *belgha* soles for eternity as punishment.

The tannery was considered both a dangerous place – as it was the entrance to the domain of the Other Ones – and a beneficial one, since skins were a symbol of preservation and fertility. Because the tanners spent their days in pits working the skins, they were said to be in contact with the unseen world of the dead and to be masters of fertility, being strong men, capable of giving a second life to dry, dead skin.

The process of tanning skins is strongly symbolic – the tanners say that the skin eats, drinks, sleeps and 'is born of the water'. When the skin is treated with lime, it is said to be thirsty; when it is treated with pigeon dung, it is said to receive *nafs*, a spirit. The *merkel* (treading) stage prepares the skin to live again, while the *takkut* of the tanning mixture is also used by women to dye their hair. At this point, the skin receives *ruh* (breath). Leather is thus born from the world of the dead and the *ighariyin*, the people of the grotto, and is fertilized in the swampy pool, the domain of the dead – who are also said to have the power to bring rain.

In the old days, the complex process of tanning would start with soaking the skins in a sort of swamp – or *iferd* – in the middle of the tannery, filled with a fermenting mixture of pigeon guano and tannery waste. Fermenting would last three days in summer, six in winter. Then the skins would be squeezed out and put to dry. Hair would be scraped off, then the skins would go into a pit of lime and argan-kernel ash. This would remove any remaining flesh or hair, and prepare the skin to receive the tanning products. The lime bath lasts 15-20 days in summer, up to 30 in winter. Then the skins are washed energetically, trodden to remove any lime, and any extra bits are cut off. Next the skins spend 24 hours in a *qasriya*, a round pit of more pigeon dung and fresh water. At this stage the skin becomes thinner and stretches. There follows soaking in wheat fibre and salt for 24 hours to remove any traces of lime and guano.

Then begins the actual tanning process. (The word *debbagh* actually means tannin.) Traditional tanneries used only plants – roots, barks and certain seeds and fruits. In Marrakech, acacia and oak bark are used, along with takkut, the ground-up fruit of the tamarisk. A water and tannin mix is prepared in a pit, and the skins get three soakings.

After this, the skins are prepared to receive the dye. They are scraped with pottery shards, beaten and coated with oil, alum and water. Then they are dyed by hand and left to dry in the sun (traditionally on the banks of the nearby Oued Issil). Finally, the skins are worked to make them smoother and more supple, stretched between two ropes and worked on smooth pottery surfaces.

Gardens

Agdal Gardens

The Agdal Gardens, stretching south of the medina, were established in the 12th century under Abd el Moumen, and were expanded and reorganized by the Saâdians. The vast expanse, over 400 ha, includes several pools, and extensive areas of olive, orange and pomegranate trees. They are in the main closed when the king is in residence, but otherwise can be visited on Fridays and Sundays between 0900 and 1800. Of the pavilions, the Dar al Baida was used by Sultan Moulay Hassan to house his harem. The largest pool, Sahraj el Hana, receives its coachloads of tourists, but at other times is a pleasant place to relax, although not to swim.

Menara Gardens

From the medina and the Agdal Gardens, Avenue de la Menara leads to the Menara Gardens, essentially an olive grove centring on a rectangular pool. A short moped hop from central Marrakech, the area is much appreciated by locals for picnics. The presence of such a large expanse of water generates a pleasant microclimate. The green-tiled pavilion alongside the pool was built in 1866. With the Atlas Mountains as backdrop, it features heavily on postcards.

Jardin Majorelle

ⓘ *Av Yacoub el Mansour, T0524-313047, www.jardinmajorelle.com, daily 0800-1800 in the summer, 40dh, plus 25dh for the museum.*

The Jardin Majorelle, also called the Bou Saf-Saf Garden, is off Avenue Yacoub el Mansour in Guéliz. This is a small tropical garden laid out in the inter-war period by a French artist, Jacques Majorelle, son of a family of cabinet-makers from Nancy who made their money with innovative art nouveau furniture. Majorelle portrayed the landscapes and people of the Atlas in large, strongly coloured paintings, some of which were used for early tourism posters. The carefully restored garden belonged to Yves St Laurent until his death in 2008 and his ashes were scattered here. Strong colours and forms are much in evidence: the buildings are vivid cobalt blue, the cactuses sculptural. Bulbuls sing in the bamboo thickets and flit between the Washingtonia palms. A green-roofed pavilion houses a small **Musée d'Art Islamique**, with a fine and easily digestible collection of objects.

The Palmeraie

Marrakech is surrounded by extensive palm groves. In the original Prost development plan of the 1920s, no building was to be higher than a palm tree. It is also illegal to cut down a palm tree – hence palms have been left growing in the middle of pavements. In recent years the Palmeraie has suffered as the urbanized area round Marrakech has expanded, and certain areas have been divided up for upmarket holiday development. Nevertheless, it is a good place for a drive or a calèche tour. Take the Route de la Palmeraie, off the N8 to Fès, to explore it.

Marrakech listings

For hotel and restaurant price codes and other relevant information, see pages 10-16.

🛏 Where to stay

Marrakech *p26, maps p32 and p37*
It is a good idea to reserve rooms, as demand for accommodation can outstrip supply in Marrakech, especially around Christmas and Easter holidays. Riads aside, the larger upmarket hotels are located in 3 areas: in the Hivernage garden city area and along the neighbouring Av Mohammed VI; in a development on the Casablanca road in the Semlalia neighbourhood; and in the Palmeraie east of the city. Hivernage is close to Guéliz, and a short taxi ride into Jemaâ el Fna in the old town.

There is a lack of stylish mid-range hotels in the medina; those that do exist are mostly grouped around Riad Zitoun el Kedim, to the southeast of Jemaâ el Fna, but they tend to fill up far in advance. There are, however, some good medium-priced hotels in Guéliz, the centre of the *ville nouvelle*.

The vast majority of cheaper hotels are 5 to 10 mins' walk from Jemaâ el Fna, in the alleys off Rue Bab Agnaou (Av Prince Moulay Rachid), Riad Zitoun el Kedim and the Kennaria neighbourhood behind the Café-Hotel de France.

Riads in the medina

Always double-check your riad reservation at peak times of year (end of year holidays, Easter, May/Jun).

€€€€ Dar Les Cigognes, 108 Rue de Berima, T0524-382740, www.lescigognes. com. Open since 2001, **Dar Les Cigognes** is a luxurious take on the riad-cum-boutique hotel. With just 11 rooms and suites, an award-winning restaurant and cooking school, full-service spa and a superb location next to the palaces, it is one of the very few riads in the old town with street access,

making it very easy to find. Emphasis on service. Part of the Sanssouci Collection.
€€€€ Le Nid, 40 Derb Saka, Mellah, T0524-382740, www.lenid.co. This luxurious modern 4-bedroom riad adjacent to the spice souks offers a 24-hr butler, personal chef, cinema room and sun terrace. Ideal for families or small groups. Part of the Sanssouci Collection.
€€€€ Maison MK, 14 Derb Sebaai, Quartier Ksar, T0524-376173, www.maison mk.com. Vibrant, bright and exceedingly hip, the 6 suites of the luxurious **Maison MK** combine traditional riad decoration standards – *tadelakt* and wrought iron – with contemporary Moroccan design elements and all mod cons. So funky is the place that even the mint teapots are brightly coloured and two-toned. The cinema room has a 2.5-m screen as well as an Xbox and you can put in advance requests for what you'd like in your minibar. Each room has iPod and mobile phone. For 22,000dh you can have the whole riad. Minimum stay of 3 nights, price includes airport transfers.
€€€€ Riad Charaï, 54 Diour Jdad, Zaouïa, T0524-437211, www.riadcharai. com. The former residence of the Pacha of Marrakech's secretary, this elegant boutique riad sleeps up to 16 people in enormous suites, of which some have twin bed arrangements. Decor is full of velvet tones and sultry low-level lighting, and lounge areas and terrace are beautiful. Service is top-notch. There's a hammam, a massage room, a spectacular, turquoise pool (4 m by 9 m – unusually large for a riad) and a huge garden patio. Situated north of the souks, it's a good 15 mins' walk to the main Jemaâ el Fna square.
€€€€ Riad El Fenn, Derb Moullay Abdullah Ben Hezzian, Bab el Ksar, T0524-441210, www.riadelfenn.com. Possibly Marrakech's most spectacularly luxurious riad, **El Fenn** also does the simple things well. The design is striking – deep red walls

coexist with more classic riad style, and a fine collection of contemporary art adorns the walls. There are 21 rooms, most of which have private fires, and one of which has a private, glass-bottomed rooftop pool, through which sunlight streams into the room below. Owned by Vanessa Branson, but run with laconic French style, **El Fenn** has some great ecological policies: it uses solar panels and has its own organic garden outside the city which provides the riad with fresh produce. There is a fine restaurant and bar, loads of cosy cushioned seating nooks and 3 pools with shaded terraces. The only danger is that once inside, you'll hardly want to venture out!

€€€€ **Riad el Ouarda**, 5 Derb Taht Sour Lakbir Taht es Sour, Zaouïa el Abbasia, T0524-385714, www.riadelouarda.com. Around 2 courtyards, the larger of which has a small pool, Ouarda has 4 double rooms and 5 suites, all with their own theme. There's a modern feel to the place; plain white walls and low furniture laid out with pebbles combine with restrained use of traditional Moroccan tiles and fabrics. Some suites have their own patio and open fireplace. Twin bed arrangements possible. Located on the northern side of the medina, it's a fair way from the majority of tourists.

€€€€ **Riad Enija**, 9 Derb Mesfioui, Rahba Lakdima, T0524-440926, www. riadenija.com. 15 rooms and suites with fabulously extravagant metal-framed and 4-poster beds around a truly jungliferous courtyard. Swiss- and Swedish-managed, every room is done in a different style, though all share a sense of exotic romance: modern European touches mix with an extravagance of tiles, arches, carved plaster and draped fabrics. Not all rooms have en suite bathrooms, though some have their own private veranda. Central location in medina and excellent service, with breakfast included. Annoyingly, prices are not shown on the website.

€€€€ **Riad Kaiss**, 65 Derb Jdid, Riad Zitoun Kedim, T0524-440141, www.riad kaiss.com. Open since 2000, **Riad Kaiss** was once a wing of the Vizier's harem. Opulent and decadent in equal measure, with 9 rooms and suites, hammam, full service spa, and pool, it's on a quiet side street just steps from Jemaâ el Fna. It also has an award-winning restaurant and cooking school. Part of the Sanssouci Collection.

€€€€ **Riad Zolah**, 114-116 Derb el Hammam, T0524-387535, www.riadzolah. com. Exemplary service sets **Zolah** apart. There are complimentary *babouches*, a mobile phone is lent to guests in case you get lost, and the welcome is warm and friendly. It's also exceptionally beautiful: one courtyard has 4 orange trees, the other a plunge pool, and the 17th-century building retains some original plasterwork. Alan Keohane's black-and-white photos of Morocco decorate the place, there's a selection of Moroccan wines, 3 rooms have working fireplaces, and spectacular silk drapes and romantic lighting add to the special atmosphere. Free Wi-Fi. Free airport transfers.

€€€€-€€€ **Riad Africa**, 94-95 Derb Sakka, Riad Zitoun Lakdim, Tel: +44(0)20-7193 2461, www. riadafrica.co.uk. Individually decorated a/c rooms, with iPod docking stations, have en suite bathrooms with *tadelakt* walls. A plunge pool is set in an attractive palm-filled courtyard. There's a fresh juice bar and rooftop garden, and a massage room with hammam. Moroccan breakfast, Wi-Fi and mobile phones provided for contacting staff whilst out are included in the price. Dinner is also available.

€€€€-€ **Equity Point Hostel**, 80 Derb el Hammam, Mouassine, T0524-440793, www.equity-point.com. 300 m from Jemaâ el Fna, this is a hostel by name but a riad in style, with lamps and arches, sofas and cushions, big mirrors and shiny red-walled bathrooms. You can stay in an en suite double for about the same price you'd pay in a riad proper (€€€€), or go budget in an 8-bed dorm (€). It's open 24/7, and breakfast and internet is included. Comprehensive online booking system.

€€€ **Dar Hanane**, 9 Derb Lalla Azzouna, T0524-377737, www.dar-hanane.com. iPod docking stations, free Wi-Fi and an honesty bar all contribute to the open, friendly attitude at this place near the Medersa Ben Youssef. There's 1 suite and 4 rooms (all with a/c), all elegantly stylish but also homely and unfussy. A superb terrace view tops the place off. English-speaking staff. If it's full, the owners have 2 more riads in the city: **Riad Tzarra** and **Dar Bel Haj**.

€€€ **Dar Mouassine**, 148 Derb Snane, Mouassine, T0524-445287, www.dar mouassine.com. Spectacular painted ceilings, lots of antiques, old pictures, books and muted natural tones give **Mouassine** a touch of sober class. It's tricky to find initially, but is located close to the main square in Moussaine. Service can be hit and miss and, though there is a/c in some rooms, it is not always working well. Meals available on request.

€€€ **Riad 72**, 72 Arset Awsel, Bab Doukkala, T0524-387629, www.riad72. com. Italian-run **Riad 72** is an exceptionally stylish riad – traditional *tadelakt* and tiles are used but the colour palette is more muted than most, with lots of greys along with splashes of red. There are only 4 rooms (all a/c), but plenty of space, with huge banana palms in the courtyard, a small splash pool, a hammam and a roof terrace with great views across the medina. There is vehicle access to this smart area in the medina and parking close by. The same people run the equally chic **Riad Due** and **Riad 12**.

€€€ **Riad el Cadi**, 86/87 Derb Moulay Abdelkader, Dabachi, T0524-378655, www.riyadelcadi.com. 14 rooms and suites around 5 courtyards in 7 conjoined houses make the cultured **Dar el Cadi** one of the medina's biggest riads. It was also one of the first riads in the city to open its doors to guests and the years of practice have

The riad experience

The riad (*maison d'hôte* or guesthouse) gives you the experience of staying in a small but fine private medina house. Prices are high for Morocco, but you get service, style and luxury in bucketloads. The often painstakingly restored houses are managed either directly by their owners or via an agency which deals with everything from reservations to maintenance. There are hundreds of riads in the city, probably around 1000, though estimates vary wildly.

Guests are met either at the airport, or the edge of the medina. Prices vary enormously, and some are extremely luxurious. Reactions to this type of accommodation are generally very positive. The riads have created a lot of work for locals (and pushed property prices up), so many feel they have a stake in the guesthouse system. (With regard to tipping, err on the generous side.)

Most riads are available to rent in their entirety, making a great base for a group or family holiday. Staff are usually included and food and entertainment (acrobats, musicians, dancers) can often be arranged.

When booking a stay in a riad in winter, check for details of heating. All riads should provide breakfast, included as part of the price, and most will also cook an evening meal on request, though advance warning is usually required. Cooler, darker ground floor rooms are preferable in summer; lighter, warmer first floor rooms in winter. Note too that, in winter, it can rain heavily in Marrakech, turning streets in the old town to muddy tracks.

What riads consider to be high season varies but always includes Christmas and Easter holidays. Rates often fall substantially outside these times. Riads usually quote their fees in euros.

Riad rental agencies

It may pay to shop around and see what is offered by riad rental agencies – they usually add a commission to the price, but they can also have special offers available. **Hôtels & Ryads**, 31 Bis, Rue Victor Massé, 75009 Paris, T+33-(0)1-42 08 18 33, www.riads.co.uk. With 64 riads in Marrakech on their books and one of the easiest to use websites, a good place to get an idea of what's available.

Riads au Maroc, 1 Rue Mahjoub Rmiza, Guéliz, T0524-431900, www.riadomaroc.com. A personalized service for both rooms in riads and whole riads from a range of 55 properties. Prices for a double room are from €45 up to €300, most are around the €70 mark.

Marrakech Riads, 8 Derb Charfa Lekbir, Mouassine, T0524-391609, www.marrakech-riads.net. Friendly and highly recommended agency with 8 excellent riads, including the simple Dar Sara and the beautiful Al Jazira. The headquarters, the beautiful Dar Cherifa, a 17th-century house converted with gallery space on the ground floor, are worth a visit in their own right (see page 57).

Villas of Morocco Immeuble Berdai, 1st floor, Guéliz, T0522-942525, www.villasofmorocco.com. For the ultimate in luxury beyond the confines of the medina, this UK agency has a portfolio of magnificent private villas in the Palmeraie and elsewhere. All are fully staffed to cater for weddings, events and family deluxe holidays. On average from around €3600 per night for exclusivity.

---

paid off. Service is efficient and friendly, and cool, simple and scholarly decoration is the order of the day. Library, Wi-Fi, tented roof terrace. Minimum stay of 3 nights. 10 mins' walk from Place Jemaâ el Fna, but there is a porter to carry your luggage on arrival/departure. The **Blue House** is ideal for families/groups (up to 4) at 3300dh per night. Closed in Ramadan.

€€€ Riad Malika, 29 Derb Arset Aouzal, Bab Doukkala, T0524-385451, www.riad malika.com. Featuring lots of eccentric old chairs and art deco touches, **Malika** is the product of years of careful tending and collecting by its French owner. The patio is thick with vegetation, shading the pool and, although reports of the quality of service are mixed, you get character in abundance. Spacious rooms, with a/c and Wi-Fi throughout. Central location in Dar el Bacha area, but quite a walk from Jemaâ el Fna.

€€€ Riad Porte Royale, Derb el Matta 84, Diour Jdad, Zaouïa Sidi bel Abbes, T0524-376109, www.riadporteroyale.com. Owned by an English writer, **Porte Royale** brings a touch of British elegance to the northern edge of the medina. There's no over-the-top decoration or wild kaleidoscope of colours here, just pristine white walls, a few carefully chosen pieces of furniture and occasional rare fabrics. The stylish reserve of the decoration serves to emphasize the beauty of the building and contributes to an atmosphere of serenity. The location is a beautiful part of the medina that few tourists reach and service is superbly friendly and attentive. Excellent value.

€€€ Riad Tizwa, Derb Gueraba 26, Dar el Bacha, T0668-190872 (Morocco) or T+44-7973-115471 (UK), www.riadtizwa.com. Stylish and good value, the Bee brothers' Marrakech riad is an elegant place near Dar el Bacha and claims to be "Marrakech's first environmentally recognized riad", sourcing produce from organic local suppliers. Well-designed without being fussy, the 6 bedrooms, primarily white with splashes of colour, open into a central courtyard with a small fountain. Huge beds are exceptionally comfortable and the dressing areas are a great design feature – bring plenty of clothes in order to make full use of the inventive hanging space behind enormous *tadelakt* headboards. Bathrooms

are luxurious, with innumerable thick towels and soft hooded dressing gowns you may never want to get out of. Wi-Fi, iPod docks and good food.

€€ Les Jardins Mandaline, 55 derb Ferrane Riad Laarouss, T0524-382295, www.lesjardins-mandaline.com. This French-run, good value riad has 8 differently decorated rooms, all with private bathrooms. There's a plunge pool and a pretty *tadelakt* hammam too. Fresh flowers punctuate the mainly white decoration, and the salon has chess and a collection of DVDs. The roof terrace doesn't have any views, but it's quiet and there are sun loungers. Excellent value, though the rooms are a bit cramped.

€€ Riad Dar Maia, 31 Derb Zouina, Riad Zitoune Jedid, T0524-376231, www.riad-dar-maia.com. Tucked into a side alley at the Bahia Palace end of Riad Zitoune Jedid, this pretty little guesthouse has 5 simple colour-themed rooms, each with an en suite shower room. There is a cosy tea salon for guests and 2 roof terraces for breakfast. The English-speaking owner and house manager are exceptional hosts. It's also a bargain.

€€ Riad Marianis, 26 derb el Firane, Riad Laarouss, T0524-383696, www.riad-marianis.com. *Tadelakt*, long narrow rooms and heritage Moroccan rugs and drapes tick all the riad boxes. There's also a good roof terrace, and excellent food is cooked to order. What sets the relaxed **Marianis** apart is the warmth of the welcome. It's also very good value. Check the website for occasional special offers.

€€ Riad tlaatawa-sitteen, 63 Derb el Ferrane, Riad Laarouss, T0524-383026, www.tlaatawa-sitteen.com. This is remarkably good value for a riad. You don't get all the polished edges that come with most riads, but you still get a stylish place to stay in the heart of the medina. Homeliness is emphasized, and the option to go to the market or to a hammam with the staff makes a stay here feel almost like being part of a Moroccan family. There's a salon with books and music, and a kitchen for guests to use. The grey-green colour scheme and Moroccan tiles give the place a young, hip feel. Nearby, the chilled **Dar Najma**, under the same management, has 3 simply styled suites (**€€€**).

Hotels in the medina
€€€€ Jardins de la Koutoubia, 26 Rue de la Koutoubia, T0524-388800, www.les jardinsdelakoutoubia.com. Close to the Koutoubia on the site of one of Marrakech's finest palaces, Dar Louarzazi, **Les Jardins** has a spectacular and elegant central courtyard with a large square pool, off which the lights sparkle at night. As well as the pool, there is a spa, 3 restaurants, an underground car park and a rooftop restaurant with great views. Its size – there are 72 rooms and suites – means that service can be a little impersonal but you're right at the heart of the action. With elevators to all floors and street-level access, this hotel is ideal for wheelchair users. Buffet breakfast is 190dh.

€€€€ La Maison Arabe, 1 Derb Assehbe, Bab Doukkala, T0524-387010, www.lamaisonarabe.com. Once one of Marrakech's best restaurants, **La Maison Arabe** is now converted into very swish accommodation, run by an Italian who grew up in Tangier. Despite its size – 12 rooms and 14 deluxe suites – there is something of a private-house atmosphere. There are 2 courtyards and most suites have private terraces and fireplace. A shuttle bus runs to the hotel's own Country Club, set in gardens just outside the city. Cookery classes are recommended, or you can just eat at the in-house restaurant or 1930s themed piano bar.

€€€€ La Mamounia, Av Bab Jedid, T0524-388600, www.mamounia.com. A Marrakech institution, the **Mamounia** was one of the first hotels in the city, built on 8 ha of gardens within the walls and a couple of mins' walk from the Koutoubia. Originally owned and run by Moroccan railways, it has been patronized by the rich and famous ever since opening in 1923. After extensive multi-million pound renovations, the hotel reopened in 2009 and is truly a magnificent homage to Moroccan architecture, design and elegance. Moroccans still talk about it in hushed, awestruck tones, and it looks set to continue as the country's most luxurious hotel for some time. If it's out of your league, you can call in for tea in the gardens for 350dh per head.

€€€€ La Sultana, 403 Rue de la Kasbah, T0524-388008, www.lasultanamarrakech. com. 5 conjoined riads make up this luxury hotel overlooking the Saâdian tombs, in the Kasbah area of the city. From the outside you'd hardly know it was there but inside 28 beautifully crafted rooms and suites open up off enormous corridors, and there are 1200 m sq of roof terrace with a bar. There's a heated pool, a jacuzzi and a *salon de massage* too. Decoration is ornate, with chandeliers, rich sultry colours and the pervasive tinkling of water.

€€€€ Les Jardins de la Médina, 21 Derb Chtouka, T0524-381851, www.lesjardinsde lamedina.com. This hotel in a refurbished palace that once belonged to a cousin of the king has 36 a/c rooms, a heated pool surrounded by trees and good restaurants. While it lacks something of the individuality of a riad, it makes up for it with an extremely high standard of service, exceptional facilities and an exalted setting, with plenty of space for lounging in grand style. There are English newspapers, a licensed bar, lots of books, beautiful gardens overlooked by fitness machines, a hammam, a beauty centre, a jacuzzi and a cookery school, where you can spend a morning learning how to make your own Moroccan tagine. Located in the Kasbah neighbourhood with easy access.

€€€€ Villa des Orangers, 6 Rue Sidi Mimoun, T0524-384638, www.villades orangers.com. At the edge of the medina, the **Villa des Orangers** is a 5-star chic hotel in a 1930s building. Carved plasterwork and tiles give it a traditional riad flavour, while televisions, pools and minibars remind you that this is much more than a *maison d'hôte*. Musicians play every night in one of the 2 courtyards, surrounded by fountains and trees. Rooms are huge and some have private terrace. Prices include many extras, such as airport transfers and tea and pastries. Check the website for special offers for multi-night stays.

€€ Hotel Ali, Rue Moulay Ismail, T0524-444979, www.hotel-ali.com. An old travellers' favourite, this large, rambling hotel is just off Jemaâ el Fna. It's a decent base for those intending to go climbing/trekking, as it is run by people from the Atlas and there are usually guides to be found hanging out here. Don't expect anything stylish; simple rooms have as many beds squeezed into them as possible, but all now have a/c and some have a balcony. Good-value restaurant and discounts for a week's stay. Fabulous views from roof terrace. No credit cards.

€€ Hotel Assia, 32 Rue de la Recette, T0524-391285, www.hotel-assia-marrakech.com. Halfway between a riad and a budget hotel, this good-value place has *tadelakt*, tiles, plants and a fountain, though service can be on the slow side. There are 26 comfortable a/c rooms, but those downstairs are a bit gloomy. Meals available on request. Currency exchange available from reception.

€€ Hotel Belleville, 194 Riad Zitoun el Kedim, T0524-426481, www.hotelbelleville.ma. 4-poster beds are squeezed tightly into some of the 9 en suite rooms in this small hotel not far from Jemaâ el Fna. There's lots of wrought iron, a pleasant roof terrace with tent and a heated Moroccan salon too. Plenty of traditional features, but a bit cluttered and untidy. Free Wi-Fi in the patio and a/c. A good budget option.

€€ Hotel Gallia, 30 Rue de la Recette, T0524-445913, www.ilove-marrakesh.com/hotelgallia. At the cheap end of the city's stylish places to stay, the **Gallia** is clean and conveniently located in a 1930s building

with a beautifully planted courtyard, a huge tree and caged birds. There's plenty of hot water and the 3 floors have carved plaster, peach-painted walls and Moroccan tiles. Though rooms aren't overly fancy, they have good beds, and breakfast is included, so it's good value. Heading down Rue Bab Agnaou from Jemaâ el Fna, it's at the end of a narrow street on the left. Popular, so reserve well in advance (by fax). English-speaking staff.

€€ Hotel Jnane Mogador, 116 Riad Zitoun el Kedim, T0524-426324, www.jnanemogador.com. So popular that management advise booking 6 months in advance, this place fills a gap in the market between grotty budget hotels and stylish but expensive riads. Theirs is a blueprint that others in Marrakech are now starting to follow, but still nobody else does it quite this well. The 17 rooms aren't large but they have attractive drapes and rugs, and en suite bathrooms. There's a pretty courtyard with a petal-filled fountain, roof terrace with spectacular views to the Koutoubia, free internet access, a hammam with massage and a salon with both a/c for summer and a fire for winter. Great location close to Jemaâ el Fna. Breakfast is 40dh.

€€ Hotel Sherazade, 3 Derb Djama, T0524-429305, www.hotelsherazade.com. Beds are big, fabrics are bold and striped, there's lots of greenery and the vibe is friendly in this hotel southeast of Jemaâ el Fna. It's spotlessly clean and the 23 rooms are arranged around large courtyards. Breakfast is an extra 50dh for a buffet on the roof terrace. The owners also have 2 bungalows for rent 14 km north of the city. The street is the 3rd narrow one on your left as you head down Riad Zitoun el Kedim from Jemaâ el Fna. Good value and very popular, so book well in advance.

€€ Sindi Sud, 109 Derb Sidi Bouloukate, T0524-443337, sindisud@hotmail.com. Just around the corner from **Hotel Médina**, this place has a room on each floor with private shower, a/c and heating, with breakfast included in the price. Other tiled standard rooms (lower end of the € category) are very clean and have basins with shared showers (5dh) on the corridors. There are some nice touches, such as decorated doors and some carved plasterwork. The roof terrace has plants and a laundry area. Even breakfast (15dh) is good value.

€ **Hotel Essaouira**, 3 Derb Sidi Bouloukate, T0524-443805. Clean, simple rooms with coloured glass, basins and mirrors. Shared bathrooms are good and clean and hot showers are included in the price. Tiles and old painted woodwork give the place some style and there are tents, plants and a kitchen on the roof terrace, assuming you can get up the steep spiral stairs. A suite would be a good option for a family.

€ **Hotel Ichbilia**, 1 Rue Bani Marine, T0524-381530. The best of the 32 rooms here have balconies overlooking the street, though these can be noisy. Beds are comfortable but there's little style. The 7 rooms with bathrooms are good value, but those without a/c or en suite bathrooms are even cheaper. No frills, but as cheap as chips. No breakfast available.

€ **Hotel La Gazelle**, 13 Rue Bani Marine, T0524-441112, hotel_gazelle@hotmail.com. The eponymous Gazelle sits on a shelf in the light and pretty courtyard of this friendly budget option south of Jemaâ el Fna. Pink walls predominate and there's a roof terrace, though the beds are rather old and sagging. Rooms have basins, some have bathrooms, otherwise shared showers on corridors.

Hotels in the ville nouvelle

€€€€ **Dar Ayniwen**, Tafrata, Palmeraie, T0524-329684, www.dar-ayniwen.com. Luxury of the ornate, antique sort is on offer at this palm grove guesthouse. Very different to the minimalist riad chic usually found in such places, the decoration creates a more lived-in, but no less elegant atmosphere. 'House cars' with drivers are available to take you wherever you desire in the city. There's a pool, extensive gardens with fruit trees, cacti and English lawn, and a hammam. Minimum stay 2 nights.

€€€€ **Dar Rhizlane**, Av Jnane el Harti, T0524-421303, www.dar-rhizlane.com. The 19 a/c rooms and suites in this Hivernage boutique hotel are decorated in the riad style but the *ville nouvelle* setting on an olive tree-lined boulevard gives an extra spaciousness you rarely find in the medina. There is also a good-sized pool and a rose garden. Some rooms have private gardens, and there is a gourmet restaurant open to non-residents. There is an air of tranquility that is normally found only in the villas of the Palmeraie, but **Dar Rhizlane** is within walking distance of the city centre. Afternoon tea is complimentary. Free Wi-Fi.

€€€ **Bab Hotel**, Corner Rue Mohammed el-Beqal and Blvd Mansour Eddahbi, T0524-435250, www.babhotelmarrakech.com. A funky new boutique hotel in the heart of Guéliz full of trendy 70s retro design. All aesthetically very pleasing and crisp, with minimalist decor and furnishings in shades of white. Roof terrace with Wi-Fi, bar and sun loungers, a small enclosed pool and stylish chill-out lounges with fluffy coloured lampshades and rag-rugs. Restaurant and bar attracts the Marrakech 'arty' types.

€€€ **Diwane**, 24 Rue Yougoslavie (just off Av Mohammed V), T0524-432216, www.diwane-hotel.com. One of the most human of the city's super-hotels, Diwane has a good pool with grassy surrounds, café and a boutique which actually sells some useful maps and books alongside the usual tourist tat. The 115 rooms are a cut above the usual big hotel standard too – they have generous desks, balconies and fridges and tiles and *tadelakt* in the bathrooms for some local style. A good option if you want a big hotel with all the trimmings and don't mind sharing it with tour groups. The Moroccan buffet dinner is worth trying, but skip the 'international' menu. 2 hammams, sauna, gym, hairdresser.

€€€-€€ **Moroccan House Hotel**, 3 Rue Loubnane, T0524-420305, www.moroccan

househotels.com. The 50 rooms in this modern hotel are decorated in a rather over-the-top recreation of riad style. There are 4-poster beds and lots of purple and bright colours, creating an overall sense of fun. There's a good pool (not heated) and a big roof terrace for breakfast, plus a more traditional hammam in the basement. Service, in contrast to the frilly decor, is staid and professional. Some tour groups. Breakfast is 59dh.

€€ **Hotel du Pacha**, 33 Rue de la Liberté, T0524-431327, www.hotelpacha.net. On a quiet corner of Marrakech's *ville nouvelle*, this 1930s hotel is a good, if old-fashioned establishment, reminiscent of colonial times with its heavy wooden panelling and ornate carved plasterwork. Ground floor rooms have been renovated with en suite marble bathrooms, and all rooms are freshly painted and decorated with Moroccan fabrics; some have small balconies. Double, twin or triple bed arrangements possible. Staff very helpful, and alcohol in the bar is an added bonuses. There's a restaurant too, with a 150dh menu, or à la carte main dishes from 60dh. All in all, good value.

€€ **Hotel Fashion**, 45 Av Hassan II, T0524-423707, fashionhotel@menara.ma. Don't be put off by the ugly exterior, or the naff name; this friendly place combines something of riad style with a convenient location and contemporary mid-sized hotel advantages such as a rooftop pool (albeit a small and rather shallow one; you may bang your knees), a hammam and a good café downstairs for breakfast. Spacious and fairly plush rooms are decked out in warm yellows and reds, with comfortable sofas, big desks and good beds. Showers have a habit of going suddenly very hot, so it may be a good idea to make use of the baths. Free Wi-Fi in reception and breakfast is included.

€€ **Ryad Mogador Opera**, Av Mohammed VI, T0524-339390, www.ryadmogador.com. Situated just across from the Theatre Royal in Guéliz, this branch 4-star link in the Ryad Mogador chain is a good option for those who want a resort-style hotel, as long as the building works next door have finished (still ongoing in 2011). There are 111 rooms here, around an octagonal central atrium with a giant chandelier. Painted wood gives a small touch of local style. Good big pool and a spa, but as with all the Ryad Mogador hotels, no alcohol is served. **Ryad Mogador Menara** offers more of the same just down the road at a 5-star grade, but avoid the **Ryad Mogador Marrakech** near Bab Doukkala. Price includes breakfast.

€ **Hotel Toulousain**, 44 Rue Tarik Ibn Ziad, Guéliz, T0524-430033, www. hoteltoulousain.com. Downstairs rooms open onto a quiet garden courtyard with climbing plants, decorated in pink and blue. There's car parking on the street (paid) and it's a friendly, laid-back place, and very handy for the excellent **Café du Livre** next door. 1st floor rooms can be hot in summer. Rooms without bathroom are cheaper, with breakfast included.

Outskirts of the city

In the Palmeraie, to the north of the centre, the old palm groves are increasingly being taken over by large, smart hotels and villa-style boutique hotels. These can feel a bit far from the action, though there is usually the advantage of large pools and luscious gardens. Many provide transport into the city centre.

€€€€ **Amanjena Resort**, Route de Ouazarzate Km 12, T0524-399000, www. amanjena.com. This is a top-end complex centring on a large reflecting pool. Featured as the palatial retreat for the girls in the film *Sex and the City II*, this luxurious accommodation starts at 9500dh per night for a 'pavilion' and goes up to 30,000dh for a 'maison' with a private pool. Everything is spectacularly grand and spacious, but, despite the use of local materials, the newness of the place is hard to hide and it therefore lacks something of the soul of a genuine riad. Nevertheless, wood-burning fires, candle lanterns, a gym, clay tennis courts and hammams make the sky-high prices a little easier to swallow, but the continental breakfast is 250dh extra.

€€€€ CaravanSerai, 264 Ouled Ben Rahmoune, T0524-300302, www.hotel caravanserai.com. Elegant and stylish, **CaravanSerai** (the word means an old roadside inn) has 13 suites, 4 rooms and 40 staff, which gives some indication of the levels of service you should expect. Pale colours and white drapes dominate, creating an atmosphere of calm, and there are vines and jacaranda trees. There's a fantastic vaulted hammam, heated pools, Wi-Fi, 2 daily city centre shuttle buses, billiards, restaurant, bar and airport transfer. Prices have been recently cut and, with frequent special offers, this is affordable luxury.

€€€€ Jnane Tamsna, Douar Abiad, Palmeraie, T0524-328484, www.jnane tamsna.com. Well away from the bustle of downtown Marrakech, the 24 rooms are spread over 5 villas in a walled herb, vegetable and fruit tree garden. The whole ensemble makes an elegant, sophisticated and peaceful place to stay. The design is traditional Moroccan, with lots of personal touches, such as old photos and furniture designed by the owner, Meryanne Loum-Martin. The roll-call of celebrity visitors bears testimony to the highly personalized service and extras, such as organic food, yoga courses, tennis coaching and 5 pools (not always heated). It's one of the best addresses in Marrakech, but the high standards come at a price, although rates include breakfast and soft drinks. Meryanne and her husband Gary, who set up the Global Diversity Foundation, are currently working on a new project, **Jnane Ylane**, a boutique hotel and natural spa that should be completed in 2014.

€€€€ Les Deux Tours, Douar Abiad, Palmeraie, T0524-329525, www.les-deux-tours.com. Out in the palm groves, this small development was originally designed by Tunisian architect Charles Boccara as second homes for Moroccans tired of the big city. The 35 traditional rooms all have balconies, are surrounded by palms and beautifully decorated in Moroccan style (tiles, fabrics and antiques). Pool suites have own private plunge pool, though there is a 300dh daily charge for heating it. There's a good communal pool too, set in verdant and extensive gardens, though there are mixed reports about the quality of service. Pick-up at Marrakech airport.

€€€€ Palmeraie Golf Palace, Circuit de la Palmeraie, T0524-368722, www. pgpmarrakech.com. The best of the behemoths in the palm groves outside Marrakech, with a frequent shuttle service into town. 5-star luxury directed towards a corporate clientele, but with spacious suites, acres of gardens, golf-course, 5 pools, tennis courts and children's programmes, it's also ideal for families. 286 rooms and 70 suites, with all expected mod cons and either a terrace or balcony. Check the website as there are deals nearly all year offering almost 50% reductions.

🍴 Restaurants

Marrakech *p26, maps p32 and p37*
Upmarket Moroccan restaurants in restored houses with garden courtyards are part of the Marrakech experience. Generally, they are indicated by a discrete wall plaque – taxi drivers know where they are, or someone from the restaurant will come to accompany you. Reservations are usually a good idea. For contemporary eating, the *ville nouvelle* has plenty of good options and, whatever your budget, you shouldn't miss the experience of dining with the locals in Jemaâ el Fna.

Medina
€€€ Dar Moha, 81 Rue Dar el Bacha, T0524-386400, www.darmoha.com. Closed Mon. One of the best medina restaurants, **Dar Moha** offers inventive Moroccan nouvelle cuisine. Try the sea bass tagine or lemon quail in filo pastry. It's easier than most to locate, being on the busy Rue

Dar el Bacha. In summer, try to get a table outside on the patio by the pool. 5-course dinner menu is 530dh per person, set lunch menus from 220dh.

€€€ Dar Zellij, Kaasour Sidi Benslimane, T0524-382627, www.darzellij.com. Converted from a 17th-century riad guesthouse to a restaurant, **Dar Zellij** now offers one of the most spectacular settings in the city in which to enjoy an evening meal. It's not easy to find but is well worth the effort. Waiters seem to float around the tree-filled courtyard in long white gowns, and the live music is subtle rather than intrusive. Tables come sprinkled with petals, there's an open fire, dark red walls, candles, enormous high ceilings, curtains and calligraphic art. The traditional Moroccan food is good too, though at times it can't quite match the extravagance of the surroundings or the service. Unimaginative vegetarian options. Set menus 300-600dh.

€€€ Ksar Essaoussan, Rue des Ksar 3, Derb el Messoudyenne, T0524-440632, www.essaoussane.com. Evenings only; closed Sun and Aug. Off Rue Fatima Zohra, where somebody will meet you with a lamp to guide you in. An intimate 18th-century patrician home where Bach plays in an antique-filled interior, **Ksar-es-saoussan** contrasts with the Las Vegas dazzle of some of the medina places. The choice of mains is limited, but it is tasty and authentic cooking. There are 3 set menus (350-550dh) including an aperitif, half-bottle of wine and soft drinks. There are good photo opportunities from the terraces. Reservations recommended.

€€€ Le Tobsil, 22 Derb Abdallah Ben Houssein, Quartier Ksar, T0524-444052. Evenings only; closed Tue. Elegant Moroccan cuisine is cooked and served with more subtlety than usual in this ochre-walled little riad. The 5-course banquet menu is fixed price and, though it's expensive at 625dh, it does include wine and aperitif. One of the longest established addresses for fine dining in the medina and

it continues to maintain its reputation for quality. Reservations are essential as there are not very many tables, and it can get a little cramped. Live gnawa music.

€€€ Villa Flore, 4 Derb Azzouz, Mouassine, T0524-391700, www.villa-flore. com. Wed-Mon, lunch and dinner. In contrast to the gaudy decor in many riad restaurants, this place is simply and quietly elegant, drawing upon an art deco palette of black, white and wine-red. The Moroccan-French food is beautifully presented, using the freshest of local ingredients. Try the *briouates* of artichoke and prawn for starters, or melt-in-the-mouth lamb. There are mixed reports about the service. Lunch menu is 220dh, dinner 330dh.

€€ Le Foundouk, 55 Souk Hal Fassi, Kaât Ben Hadid, T0524-378190, www.foundouk. com. Tue-Sun 1200-2400. For those for whom insipid, overcooked tagines have become a chore, the succulent, well-spiced versions here will be something of a welcome surprise. Near the Medersa Ben Youssef, the licensed **Foundouk**, in a converted riad, is one of the most elegant restaurants in Marrakech. There are roses in glasses on the tables, contemporary art and mirrors on the walls, and modern jazz plays while a white, dark brown and burgundy colour scheme gives the place an air of contemporary sophistication. As well as the tagines (for around 130dh), there's European food too, and vegetarians can find plenty of choice in the starters to make up an entire meal. Evening reservations recommended.

€€ Le Jardin, 32 Souk El Jedld, Sidi Abdelaziz, T0524-378295, www.lejardin.ma. Daily 0900-2300. This large courtyard restaurant enclosed in a 17th-century mansion is 2 steps away from its sister, **Terrasse des Épices**. Under the same ownership and direction, it offers snacks, salads or light meals all day with some enticing vegetarian options. In summer there are outdoor screenings of arthouse movies in the garden, while in winter you can enjoy a meal in front of the crackling fireplace. Alcohol licence pending.

€€ Les Terrasses de l'Alhambra, Jemaâ el Fna, T0524-427570. Daily 0800-2300. Almost opposite the **Café de France** is this popular contemporary place for reasonably priced pasta, pizzas and salads. The latter are a good option, including smoked salmon and avocado. If you're in the mood for something more Moroccan, tagine and *pastilla* feature too. It's a smarter venue than many of the places around the square and has a loungey atmosphere and terraces with fab views over the square. Also good for a drink or ice-cream stop during the day. Its prime ringside location means it gets very crowded regardless of food quality or service, so don't expect too much on that front. No alcohol.

€€ Le Tanjia, 14 Derb J'did – Hay Essalam, Mellah, T0524-383836. Daily 0800-0100. Describing itself as an oriental brasserie, Le Tanjia brings something of chic Paris to the Marrakech medina; dark wood round tables and leather chairs are combined with Moroccan lanterns and palms. Food is high-quality Moroccan, with unusually good salads and vegetarian options. The terrace or the ground floor bar are good spots for a drink at any time of day. Easy to find near La Place des Ferblantiers and vehicle access to the door. Unfortunately since changing ownership in recent times, the standards have slipped.

€€ Terrasse des Épices, 15 Souk Cherifa, Sidi Abdelaziz, T0524-375904, www. terrassedesepices.com. Daily 1200-2300. From the owners of the successful **Café des Épices**, the titular terrace is a surprisingly expansive and open space on the first floor of a building in the middle of the souks. Comfortable, shaded tables and private booths are spaced around the edge and, in the evening, it becomes especially atmospheric, as the sun sets and lanterns light the place. The food is excellent; as well as a traditional 100dh Moroccan menu (lunch only), there are inventive options, such as caramalized prunes with goat's cheese crème fraiche. No alcohol.

€€-€ Les Premices, Jemaâ el Fna, T0524-391970. At the southeast edge of the square, a bit away from the main action, Les Premices is a cut above much of its competition. There are 2 levels of terrace overlooking the square or you can sit inside. Try the tasty European dishes, such as mozzarella salad or fried sole, or go for standard Moroccan tagines or couscous from around 70dh. Patchy service. No alcohol.

€ Chez Bahia, 206 Rue Riad Zitoun el Kedim, just off Jemaâ el Fna, T0524-378946. Being just off Jemaâ el Fna, **Chez Bahia** gets fewer tourists and also offers better value than some of its competitors right on the square. Tagines are only 30-50dh, and it's also a good spot for breakfast, with freshly cooked pancakes and *bisara*. It's clean, bright, basic, good value and very Moroccan. Call by and order in advance some house specialities, such as spicy aubergine tagine or pigeon *pastilla*. No alcohol.

€ Chez Chegrouni, Jemaâ el Fna. Just to the left of the **Café de France**, Chez Chegrouni is well-known for its good couscous. That, combined with its seats out front and upstairs terrace, means that it's popular, and you'll have to turn up early for the best seats. It's still good value though: a vegetable couscous only 40dh. Vegetarians will be glad to know they do not use meat stock in the vegetable dishes. No alcohol.

€ Earth Café, 2 Derb Zawak, Riad Zitoune Kedim, T0661-289402, www.earthcafe marrakech.com. Daily 1100-2300. The first of its kind in Marrakech and a welcome boost for vegetarians. Organic, vegan and totally animal-friendly food, with Asian influences, served in a colourful courtyard bedecked with paper lanterns. An array of freshly picked salads, such as beetroot salad with goat's cheese, or *pastilla* stuffed with pumpkin and courgette. No alcohol.

€ Jemaâ el Fna food stalls, one of Marrakech's great experiences, eating in Jemaâ el Fna is not to be missed. Piles of salads and steaming tagines are set up under hissing gas lamps from early evening

Café culture

Around Jemaâ el Fna there are lots of cafés which exist primarily because of their terraces overlooking the square. None are licensed, and none would be great cafés in other locations, but they are all rightfully popular, especially late in the afternoon, for the opportunity they offer to survey the frenzy below from the relative calm of a terrace. As a response to the hordes of tourists coming up to these cafés just to take photos, many will only let you onto their terraces after you've bought a drink. **Café de France** has several levels and an excellent panorama over the square and the medina beyond.

Café Glacier Le Grand Balcon, on the southeast edge of the square, has perhaps the best views of sunset through the rising smoke from the food stalls below. **Les Terrasses de l'Alhambra**, just opposite the Café de la France, is a strategic meeting place near the entrance to the souks and just beyond the mayhem of the foodstalls. Good views from the top terrace, page 56.

In Guéliz, head to the modern **Marrakech Plaza** at Place du 16 Novembre for people-watching from French-style brasserie-cafés, or spot celebrities during the annual Marrakech Film Festival from the cafés along **Avenue Mohammed VI**.

onwards. Each stall has a different variety of cooked food, from sheep heads to snails to fried fish to bowls of soup. It is best to go for the food cooked to order while waiting, and the most popular places obviously have a faster turnover of food. In general, however, eating here is no less safe than in most Moroccan restaurants, and there are rarely any problems. Walking along between the stalls is an experience in itself – you will be cajoled onto benches from all sides by young Moroccans who have somehow picked up a surreal line in mock cockney patter. Don't miss the stalls selling harira soup, served with dates and *gateaux de miel* for 9dh, or fresh fried fish at stall No 14.

€ Nid'Cigogne, 60 Rue de la Kasbah, T0524 382092, Opposite the Saâdian tombs, you climb 2 flights of stairs to reach this roof-terrace restaurant-café, serving good salads and kefta sandwiches. The *salade Maroc* is especially varied and generous for 20dh, and service is continuous 0900-2100. It makes a very handy lunch spot, and you can peer straight across the road into the nests of the eponymous storks. No alcohol.

€ Tiznit, 28 Souk el Kassasabine, just off Jemaâ el Fna, T0524-427204. Daily 0800-2300. Just a few doors from **Chez Chegrouni**, heading away from the square, you'll spot a building that juts out a few feet from the main façade. Up the steep tiled steps you'll enter a tiny restaurant jammed with a few plastic tables and locals tucking into the best and cheapest rabbit tagine in town for just 35dh. Closed during Ramadan. No alcohol.

Cafés and patisseries

Café des Épices, 75 Rahba Kedima, T0524-391770, www.cafedesepices.net. Daily 0800-2000. The open space of Rahba Kedima (the Spice Square), thronged with hat, basket and live reptile sellers, makes a great setting for the medina's best café. In a small and usually overflowing building, it offers good sandwiches and salads over 3 floors. The roof terrace is especially popular. Herbal teas also served. Free Wi-Fi.

Dar Cherifa, 8 Derb Charfa Lakbir, Mouassine, off Rue Mouassine, T0524-426463. Daily 1200-1900. Hard to find and when you do you'll probably need to ring the bell to be let in, but that adds to the rarefied air of this gallery café in a tall, spacious riad. Downstairs is a contemporary art space, while the quiet café is on the roof terrace upstairs and serves mint tea and saffron coffee. There are 2 lunch menus (90dh/120dh). Look out for occasional cultural evenings.

Patisserie Les Princes, 32 Rue de Bab Agnaou (also known as Av Prince Moulay Rachid), T0524-443033. Daily 0600-2230. On the pedestrian street south of Jemaâ el Fna, Les Princes has an excellent selection of pastries and petits fours, though the ice creams aren't great. Mint teas come in different varieties in a *salon du thé* at the back.

Riad Yima, 52 Derb Aarjane, Rahba Lakdima, T0524-391987, www.riadyima. com. Daily 0900-1800. Formerly run as a guesthouse, this place is now a small café, gallery and boutique full of quirky pop-art charm. Created by artist, photographer and designer, Hassan Hajjaj, the space is filled with his humorous recycled objets d'art and is tucked down a side-alley near the **Café des Epices**. Serves herbal teas, a variety of coffees and organic fruit juices.

Souk Café, 11 Derb Souk Jdid, Sidi Abdelaziz (near Rue Riad Larousse), T0662-610229. Daily 1100-2300. Tricky to find in the northern twists of the souks, but well worth stopping by for a fruit smoothie on the terrace of this stylishly converted old house. Cinnamon-coloured *tadelakt* walls, colourful textiles and authentic Moroccan food served throughout the day. At night the intimate restaurant comes alive with belly dancers, and customers can discreetly bring their own wine/beer.

Ville nouvelle *map p32*

While Marrakech's medina restaurants serve mostly Moroccan food, the *ville nouvelle* has a much wider range of eating and (especially) drinking options. Guéliz (the main *ville nouvelle* area) also has some good cafés, old-fashioned and modern, straight-laced and alternative, many of which also make good eating spots.

€€€ La Trattoria, 179 Rue Mohammed el Bequal, T0524-432641, www.latrattoria marrakech.com. Open evenings only from

1830. The city's smartest Italian restaurant, this place is on a leafy side street in the heart of Guéliz and oozes elegance and romance. There's a lush garden terrace for pre-dinner drinks and an excellent selection of wines. The kitchen serves up scrumptious Italian cuisine, from sun-dried tomato and mozzarella tartlets to curried monkfish with pineapple and asparagus. Reservations advisable.

€€ Al Fassia Guéliz, 55 Blvd Zerktouni, T0524-434060, www.alfassia.com. Wed-Mon 1200-2230. This excellent Moroccan restaurant is run by a women's cooperative, and all the staff, once you're past the doorman, are female. You can dine à la carte, and there's an excellent choice of tagines – for example, lamb with aubergine and chicken with caramelized pumpkin – for 130dh. Other good options include vegetable couscous and seafood *pastilla* and there's a long wine list too. The interior is elegant, with silk tablecloths and napkins, snug corners and a central area where sunlight filters down in daytime. Reservations recommended. Due to demand, a second **Al Fassia** has been opened in nearby Aguedal, though locals still say Guéliz is the best of the two.

€€ Bistro Thai, 8 Av Oued el Makhazine (opposite **Royal Tennis Club**), T0524-457311. Oriental fusion of Thai, Japanese and Vietnamese cuisine in stylish surroundings. Diners can go for the elegant sunken lounge area, sit up at the sushi bar surveying the chef at work or take a low table out on the wooden decked terrace that looks onto the street. Deliciously fragrant Thai curries, or dramatic flaming wok creations, loads of tasty nibbles, dim sum and steamed rice. Create your own variations ,choosing which meat you want with which style of sauce. Licensed bar and cocktails. The plateau of tasty starters includes satay, *nems* and tiny spring rolls and is enough for 2 people, 130dh.

€€ Catanzaro, 11 Rue Tarak Ibn Ziad, next to **Hotel Toulousain**, T0524-433737. Closed Sun. An Italian that's a bit of a Marrakech institution, with excellent wood-fired pizzas and pastas alongside other more complex dishes and meat grills. Reservations are a good idea, but you can usually also turn up and queue. Rustic charm, lively atmosphere and busy with locals and tourists for both lunch and dinner. Good value, with pizzas at 55dh and good Moroccan wines priced from 160dh per bottle.

€€ Kechmara, 3 Rue de la Liberté, T0524-422532, www.kechmara.com. Mon-Sat 0730-midnight. Like a very cool contemporary café with a good wine list and exciting food, **Kechmara** is unlike almost all other eating options in Marrakech. The tea menu includes blue and green varieties from Vietnam, and there are omlettes and panini for daytime stops. It's the evening when the place really buzzes, though, with Marrakech's bright young things sitting on designer plastic chairs ordering contemporary European food of the highest order. Live music at the weekends, art exhibitions and a shaded roof terrace bar to escape from all the cigarette smoke. Moroccan Flag beer on tap.

€€ Le Bagatelle, 103 Rue de Yougoslavie, T0524-430274, www.bagatellemarrakech. over-blog.com. Daily 0900-2300. Re-opened in 2010, this French brasserie-style restaurant is a favourite with the large expat community and has been popular since it first opened in 1949. Art-nouveau styling, long rows of tables with bentwood chairs and cushion-backed booths, potted plants and loads of old photos give an authentic bistro effect and almost obliterate any sense of the Marrakech street outside. The appetising menu includes trout meunière and quail with raisins and cinnamon. The lunch menu at 110dh is exceptional value and, with free Wi-Fi too, you could make it a working lunch and not feel guilty.

€€ Le Carioca, 120 Rue Mohammed Bequal, T0524-431485, www.lecarioca. marrakech.com. Mon-Sat 1200-1600 and 1900-0100. The newest restaurant in town is run by a Moroccan with a passion for Brazilian cooking and South American

music. Hey presto! Churrasco barbecued meats roasted on a spit and carved at your table, served with salads and live latin music. As much as you can eat for 230dh and lighter lunches from around 180dh. The bar is open to non-diners and serves tequila slammers and cocktails from 60dh.

€€ Pizzeria Niagara, Route de Targa (take a taxi), T0524-449775. Open evenings only. Generally considered Marrakech's best pizza place, Niagara is not exactly central; it's probably worth taking a taxi to get you out to the Lycée Victor Hugo neighbourhood at the far end of Av Mohammed V. Gets crowded in the evenings with local families dining on the street-front covered terrace and serves alcohol at reasonable prices. The chocolate profiteroles are to die for! It's one of a clutch of pizzerias on the same strip, so if you can't get a spot, there are others nearby. Take a moment to stroll along the street outside to admire the sculpted tree trunks.

€€ Rotisserie de la Paix, 68 Rue Yougoslavie, T0524-433118. Daily 1200-1500 and 1900-2300. Bow-tied waiters bustle around this popular spot, offering good, freshly grilled meat with a few fish options. There are also pizzas and tagines on the menu, but the whole point is really the meat or grilled fish. In the summer the garden fills up quickly with a mix of expats and tourists, plus a resident peacock, and in winter there's an open fire inside. Service can be hit and miss.

€ Restaurant Al Bahriya, 75 Av Moulay Rachid, T0524-846186. Daily 1000-midnight. Just round the corner behind **Café de la Poste** you'll find this street-restaurant, and it's usually packed with Moroccans. Fresh fish, prawns, calamares all fried in batter and served up with wedges of lime and spicy olives. A large mixed plate of fish and chips costs just 35dh. Cash only.

Cafés and patisseries

Café du Livre, 44 Rue Tarik Ben Ziad, T0524-432149, www.cafedulivre.com. 0930-2100 Mon-Sat. Despite the name, **Café du Livre**

is a fully fledged restaurant as well as a café. Unfortunately the standard of cuisine has declined drastically in recent years, but the chocolate-orange tart with good flavoursome coffee is still divine. There are books on Moroccan arts and culture to browse, second-hand novels in English and French for sale, and the free Wi-Fi makes this a popular place for informal business meetings amongst expats. Low ceilings and cigarette smoke are a problem. It's also a good place to pick up information about what's going on in the city. Off a courtyard next to **Hotel Toulousaine**. Alcohol served.

Café Les Négociants, on the corner of Av Mohammed V and Blvd Mohammed Zerktouni, T0524-435762. Daily 0700-2300. In Guéliz, this busy intersection has popular cafés on each side, but this is the granddaddy, an old-timer still at the heart of *ville nouvelle* life and the place to come for important conversations, for long, lingering mint teas and to watch the world go by.

Grand Café de la Poste, corner of Blvd El Mansour Eddahbi and Av Imam Malik, T0524-433038, www.grandcafedelaposte. com. Daily 0800-0100. Built in 1925, the extravagant **Grand Café** has immaculately restored 1920s colonial styling and a very pleasant outdoor terrace under umbrellas. It's a place people come to be seen but they pay inflated prices for the privilege. Alcohol served.

Kaowa, 34 Rue Yves Saint Laurent (opposite Jardins Majorelle), T0524-330072. Daily 0900-1900. There are potted bamboo plants and a wooden deck terrace outside, or a bright modern interior where you can tuck into fresh organic salads, tasty wraps and fruit smoothies. Nutritious and delicious for a healthy snack.

Le 16, Pl du 16 Novembre, T0524-339670. Daily 0700-midnight. This is one of a new breed of café-restaurant in Marrakech. Its lime-green umbrellas spilling onto the central Pl du 16 Novembre are almost unmissable in the *ville nouvelle*. Worth a visit for its fantastic (and often very imaginative)

ice creams and fruit juices. It also makes an excellent lunch spot, with good salads and light meals. Alcohol served.

Vlème Avenue, Residence Palm d'Or, Av Mohammed VI (corner of Blvd Mohammed Zerktouni), T0524-422388. Daily 0700-midnight. On a busy junction at the edge of Guéliz is this modern café that serves a great value full Moroccan breakfast for 35dhs: harira soup, m'smen pancakes, boiled egg, fruit juice and coffee. Also on offer are salads, paninis, pasta and light meals, and there's shaded seating with external a/c for the heat of summer. Set back from the road is a garden with tables, and something of an attraction are the family of ducks that have taken up residence in the small pond.

🎶 Bars and clubs

Marrakech *p26, maps p32 and p37*
Dedicated bars are thin on the ground in the city – your best bet for a drink is often somewhere that also functions as a licensed restaurant and stays open late, or the bars within most of the hotels. There are a few sleazy side-street bars in Guéliz around Rue Mauritanie and very expensive bars inside the city's many nightclubs.

Azar, Rue Yougoslavie (corner with Av Hassan II), Guéliz, T0524-430920, www.azar-marrakech.com. Daily 1930-0100. Stylish oriental lounge-bar with chilled world-music mix and occasional live Arabic singers. Plenty of woven carpets, candlelight and exotic ambience. Cocktails, wines and beers served with Mediterranean-themed food also available in the Moroccan-Lebanese restaurant downstairs.

Bar L'Escale, Rue Mauritania. Mon-Sat 1100-2230. A gritty, all-male environment, this bar is famed for its charcoal-grilled *coquelet* and chips with your Flag beer. Beers and some spirits served, but not for consumption at the outdoor tables.

Café Arabe, 184 Rue Mouassine, T0524-429728, www.cafearabe.com. Daily

1200-2300. Conveniently located on one of the main routes through the medina, this café offers good, if slightly unimaginative, Moroccan and Italian fare on the ground floor in a lush riad setting. Upstairs is where **Café Arabe** really comes into its own, with a rare medina bar and a relaxing rooftop terrace.

Kosybar, 47 Pl des Ferblantiers, T0524-380324. Daily 1200-0100. On several levels on the square traditionally taken up by Marrakech's metal workers, Kosybar functions as a restaurant and café but its roof terrace is a great place to hang out with a drink at sunset. The food is nothing special, cocktails are expensive at around 100dh, but bottles of Moroccan wine are reasonably priced from 150dh. Live music Thu-Sat.

Le Comptoir Darna, Av Echouhada, T0524-437702, www.comptoirdarna.com. Daily 1600-0200. Muted lighting and elegant waitresses in caftans set the tone for this popular, if pricey, drinking spot. There's a mediocre restaurant too but the licence, the live music, the belly dancers and the weekend DJs make it better suited to late-night cocktails. There's even a little boutique.

Pacha, Blvd Mohammed VI, T0524-388400, www.pachamarrakech.com. Daily 2000-0200. A big dancefloor, laid-back bars, chill-out lounge, restaurant and pool. Claims to be the biggest club in Africa. Hefty drinks prices with bottled beers starting at 100dh (admission price of 200dh includes 1 drink).

Sky Bar, La Renaissance Hotel, Av Mohammed V (corner with Blvd Mohammed Zerktouni), Guéliz, T0524-337777, www.renaissance-hotel-marrakech.com. On the 7th floor of the newly refurbished **Renaissance Hotel**, this trendy outdoor bar has the highest vantage point of anywhere in the city and a 360-degree panorama that makes the sky-high prices justifiable.

SO Night Lounge, Sofitel, Rue Haroun Errachid, Hivernage, T0524-425601, www.sofitel.com. Daily 2000-0200. More sophisticated than Pacha, this place comprises a restaurant and club with live music and DJs every night. Chill-out lounges

under a pergola in the garden where you can enjoy fresh-fruit cocktails. It's a smart affair and entry costs 200dh (including 1 drink).

Teatro, Hotel Es Saadi, Av El Kadissa, T0664-860339, www.theatromarrakech.com. Daily 2000-0200. Top DJs spin their stuff at this hip club in an ex-theatre in the Hivernage district. Hard house music is the main dramatic theme.

● Entertainment

Marrakech *p26, maps p32 and p37*
Casinos
Grand Casino de la Mamounia, at the **Mamounia Hotel**, Av Bab Jedid, T0524-448811, www.grandcasinomamounia.com. Open 2100-0400. 20 live games and 200 gambling machines in a grand art deco setting. Smart-casual dress code, no jeans or trainers.

Cinemas
The major cinemas showing films in French are the **Colisée**, Blvd Mohammed Zerktouni, T0524-448893 and the **Megarama**, Av Mohammed VI, T0890-102020, a 9-screen complex behind the **Pacha club.** Try also the **L'Institut Français**, Route de Targa, Guéliz, T0524-446930, www.ifm.ma.

Cultural and language centres
Instituto Cervantes, Av Mohammed V, Guéliz (the furthest end from Koutoubia), T0524-422055, www.marrakech.cervantes.es. Spanish cultural and language school, with occasional concerts, films, exhibitions and special events.

Institut Français, Route de la Targa, Guéliz, Tue-Sat 1000-1230 and 1500-1900 (library). With a recommended café, open-air theatre and pleasant garden, the French Institute shows films and holds exhibitions and other cultural events. The library has a small stock of books and films in French on Morocco-related subjects. Café open Tue-Sat 0900-1900.

☺ Festivals

Marrakech *p26, maps p32 and p37*
Jul The Festival National des Arts
Populaires (www.marrakechfestival.com)
brings together traditional regional music
and dance troops from all over Morocco
and some international acts.
Dec The Festival International du Film
de Marrakech (www.festivalmarrakech.
info) is held annually and attracts the stars
of Hollywood and world cinema for a truly
glitzy gathering.

○ Shopping

Marrakech *p26, maps p32 and p37*
Crafts, fabrics and clothes
Marrakech is a shopper's paradise. Craft
production has taken off in a big way, with
a range of new products, notably in metal
and ceramic, being added to classic leather
and wood items. The influence of the
international decorator set can clearly be felt.
Close to the Dar el Bacha, in the Bab Doukkala
neighbourhood, are plenty of antique dealers
and, in Guéliz, the keen shopper will find
chic boutiques with clothing, fine leather
and other items. Prices in Guéliz are fixed
and more expensive than the medina. A feel
for prices can also be gained by visiting the
workshops in the large craft training centre
(L'Ensemble Artisanale), on the right past the
Koutoubia as you head to Guéliz. Here, again,
prices are non-negotiable, and slightly more
expensive than in the old city. In a very short
time you can see people at work at practically
all the main crafts, including embroidery,
ceramic mosaic and basketry, felt hats, wood
painting and slipper making. However, it's
a tame experience compared to the sights
and sounds of the souks.

In the medina, prices are of course
negotiable. If you can approach the process
as buying non-essential, decorative items
and are prepared to walk away, it is likely
to be less painful and you'll probably get
a better deal. Keep a sense of humour

(remember how absurd it all is when some
salesman whom you met 5 mins ago
reasons that "you are not my friend because
you don't want to buy from me." Always be
polite, and you may come away with some
bargains. You might even enjoy it.

Good items to buy in Marrakech include
thuya wood boxes (though Essaouira is
the real home of this craft), painted wood
mirrors and side tables, ceramics, carpets,
leather bags and *babouches* (shoes/slippers).
Hand-woven baskets and woolly hats from
the women in the Rahba Lakdima and
Jemaâ el Fna can be got at bargain prices.
Sidi Ghanem, a few kilometres on Rte de
Safi, best reached by taxi or bus No 15,
www.sidighanem.net. Open Mon-Fri. If
you're in the market for serious home
decoration, you may want to take a trip
out of town to Sidi Ghanem 'industrial zone',
where lots of Moroccan contemporary
designers have outlets, focusing on home
interiors, candles, designer furniture, crafts
and fashion. Their main income is from
exports but most are also open to visitors.

Medina The souks can be confusing for
shopping. Originally each souk specialized
in one type of product but this system has
largely broken down on the main tourist drag
(Souk Semmarine and its continuation, Souk
el Kebir) up to the area around the Medersa
Ben Youssef. There are shops specializing in
slippers, traditional gear, wood and ceramics,
and a number of large antique shops.

If you enter the souks from opposite the
Café de France in Jemaâ el Fna you will
pass olive stalls and mint sellers on your
right, bend round to the right and you'll
find yourself in the eastern corner of a small
square called Bab Fteuh. Straight in front
of you is the (relatively) wide, paved **Souk
Semmarine**. There are some big antique
shops and carpet emporia here, some of
them very expensive. **Rahba Kedima**, a rare
open space off to the right (about 200 m up
Souk Semmarine), also has some interesting
small shops, as well as the **Café des Épices**.

Haggling

Part of the fun of shopping in the medina is the haggling that comes with every purchase. To buy in the souks you will have to engage in the theatre and the mind games of the haggle.

In order to come out of the process happy, there are some things to bear in mind. Don't get too hung up on the idea of 'a good price'. The best price is the one you are happy to pay. Have one in mind before you start and don't go above it. Be prepared to walk away if the price is too high – whatever you're buying, there will almost certainly be another stall around the corner selling the same thing.

Be friendly and polite but firm and don't suggest a price you would be prepared to pay for anything you're not sure you want. Once you start talking numbers, you are in negotiation and you may find it hard to extricate yourself. The price you are first quoted might be twice as much as the seller is prepared to accept, but there is absolutely no firm rule about this. A decent starting point from the buyer's point of view is to take about a half to a third off the amount you'd be prepared to pay and start by offering that.

As a very rough guide, and depending on quality, size, etc, expect to pay these sort of prices: *babouches* 50-150dh; leather bag 200-400dh; teapot 50-200dh (more for silver); spices 30-60dh per kg; pouffe 150-450; blanket 300-600dh.

Carpet-buying can be especially complex and has many potential pitfalls – don't be too swayed by offers of mint tea/declarations of antiquity/the years of hard toil the seller's elderly aunt spent making it.

Further on, Souk Semmarine successively becomes **Souk el Kebir**, **Souk el Najjarine** and, under a wooden lintel, **Souk Chkaïria**. Leather goods can be bought here.

The other reasonably major route through the souks is **Rue Mouassine**, which also runs north-south from the western end of Bab Fteuh, past the Mosque Mouassine. You can also get here by entering the souks next to Café Argana on Jemaâ el Fna. **Rue Dar el Bacha**, the street running west out towards Bab Doukkala, has many interesting antiques and jewellery shops.

Akbar Delights, Pl Bab Fteuh, T0671-661307, www.akbardelights.com. Tue-Sun 0900-1900. Stunningly embroidered, beaded and bejewelled fabrics, tunics and decorative accessories. Showroom and outlet also in Guéliz at 42c Rue de la Liberté, together with sister company, **Moor** (see below) selling similar beautiful crafted items for the home, but in pastel shades.
Assouss Argane, 94 Mouassine (entrance on Rue Sidi el Yamami), T0524-380125, www.assoussargane.com. Daily 0900-1800. Authentic and undiluted Moroccan argan oil and beauty products, direct from a women's co-operative near Essaouria.
Beldi, 9-11 Rue Laksour (entrance on Rue Mouassine near Bab Fteuh), T0524-441076. Daily 0930-1300 and 1600-1900. This well-known *maison de haute couture* has a fine selection of traditionally tailored caftans, slippers and bags, mainly for women. Waistcoats and flowing shirts for men. High quality at reasonable prices. Credit cards accepted.
Khartit Mustapha, 3 Fhal Chidmi, Rue Mouassine, T0524-442578. Daily 0800-2100. Specializing in baubles, bangles and beads, Mustapha is the friendly owner of this Berber jewellery shop. He can make necklaces and bracelets to order using the semi-precious stones and colourful beads (once used as currency) that he also sells by weight. Credit cards accepted.
KifKif, 8 Derb Laksour, T0661-082041 (mob), www.kifkifbystef.com. Colourful textiles,

jewellery, toys and funky leather bags, selected by expat designer. Manufactured by local crafts workers.

Le Trésor des Nomades, 142-144 Rue Bab Doukkala, T0524-385240. Daily 0900-1930. Run by Mustapha Blaoui, this is a warehouse chock-full of treasures: lanterns, carved wooden doors, goatskin-covered chests in fantastic shapes, touareg woven mats, kilims, antique *babouches* and much more. There's no sign outside, but look for the large double wooden doors. Shipping available.

Ministero del Gusto, 22 Derb Azzouz (off Rue Sidi el Yamami), T0524-426455, www.ministerodelgusto.com. Open Mon-Fri. More of a gallery space than a shop, though everything is for sale. One-off furniture creations, jewellery, paintings and vintage clothing displayed within an extraordinary multi-level building full of earthy textures and organic shapes.

Palais Saadiens Tapis,16 Rue Moulay Taïb Ksour (off Rue el Ksour), T0524-445176. Daily 0900-1900. An enormous stock of carpets from all regions of Morocco. Accepts credit cards.

Guéliz There are quite a few souvenir shops and shops selling clothes and luggage on **Av Mohammed V**. There are number of little boutique-type places on **Rue de la Liberté**, **Rue Mauritanie** and **Rue Sourya**, all of which cut across Av Mohammed V between Pl du 16 Novembre (Marrakech Plaza) and Pl Abdelmoumen Ben Ali (**Café Negoçiants** landmark). Also have a quick trawl along the streets around **Rue Mohammed Bequal** (turn left just after the restaurant La Taverne, which itself is almost opposite the **Cinéma Colisée**). At the new **Marrakech Plaza** on Pl du 16 Novembre are branches of major European chains where young Marrakchis pay high prices for western labels such as Zara, Etam, Mango, Dior and more.

33 Rue Majorelle, 33 Rue Yves Saint Laurent, T0524-314195. Opposite the Jardin Majorelle, this smart new shop has a selection of quality clothing, jewellery

and gifts from the new wave of Moroccan designers. Art gallery also attached.

Alrazal, 55 Rue Sourya, T0524-437884, www.alrazal.com. Mon-Sat 0930-1300 and 1530-1930. Exquisite hand-made clothing for children that's somewhere between fancy dress box and party outfit. Silk-embroidered miniature caftans and Ali Baba pants in a rainbow of colours. Smiles aplenty.

Galerie le Caftan, Immeuble 100, No 2, Rue Mohammed Bequal, T0661-765260. Almost opposite the **Galerie Birkemeyer**. As the name suggests, a good choice of upmarket traditional women's gear made to order on the premises. Beautiful *babouches* with a modern touch.

Lun'art Gallery, 106 Rue Mohammed Bequal, T0524-447266. Mon-Sat 0930-1300 and 1530-1930. African masks and carved wooden figures, bronze sculpted curios, hessian wall-hangings and treasures from sub-Saharan Africa. Credit cards accepted and shipping available.

Moor, 42c Rue de la Liberté, Apt 47, 1st floor, T0671-661307, www.akbardelights. com. French elegance with Moroccan influence. Pale shades dominate for lamps, house-wares, textiles and cool linen tunics.

Naturelle d'Argan, 5 Rue Sourya, T0524-448761. Open 0930-1300 and 1500-1800. Beauty products and other argan oil-based products, as well as a carefully chosen smattering of handicrafts, such as the exquisite inlaid teaspoons found in several riads in the city.

L'Orientaliste, 11 and 15 Rue de la Liberté, T0524-434074. Mon-Sat 0900-1230 and 1500-1930. Ceramics and perfumes, paintings and semi-antiques.

Books

Marrakech is not the most bookish of towns. Nevertheless, there are a few shops where you can stock up on large coffee table books, maps and recent Moroccan fiction in French. It's also worth trying the **Café du Livre** in Guéliz (page 59). Foreign newspapers, a day or two old, can be bought from the

stands along Av Mohammed V – the one next to tourist information has a good selection – and in the large hotels.
Librairie Chatr, 19/21 Av Mohammed V, T0524-447997. Under the arcades at the top end of Av Mohammed V, near the Shell station and the intersection with Rue Abd el Krim el Khattabi. The best choice of books in the city, from coffee table books to novels in English and Atlas Mountain guidebooks (in French).
Librairie Dar El Bacha, 2 Rue Dar el Bacha, T0524-391973. A small but well-stocked shop in the medina, with maps and guidebooks on its shelves.

Supermarkets
Aswak Assalam, opposite the bus station at Bab Doukkala. No alcohol.
Hypermarché Marjane, on the Casablanca road. Stocks just about everything including electrical goods, clothes, household items, food and alcohol. (Non-Moroccans can buy alcohol here during Ramadan).

Country markets
Markets outside Marrakech serve local needs, although there are inevitably a number of persistent trinket pushers. Men from the mountain villages come down on mule, bicycle and pick-up truck to stock up on tea and sugar, candles and cigarettes, agricultural produce, maybe have a haircut or even get a tooth pulled. This is the place to sell a sheep, discuss emigration, or a land sale. There may be some Islamists peddling cassettes of sermons, perfumes and religious texts. At such markets, the difference in living standards between the town and the countryside really hits home. The markets are dusty, rough-and-ready places where people pay with the tiny brass coins hardly seen in the city. You really feel that people are living from the land, and realize how hard drought can hit them.

Country market days as follows: Mon **Tnine**; Tue **Amizmiz, Tahanaoute, Ait Ourir**; Wed **Tirdouine**; Thu **Ouirgane, Setti Fatma,** **El Khemis**; Fri **Aghmmat, Tameslohte**; Sat **Asni**; Sun **Chichaoua, Sidi Abdel Ghiat**.

◑ What to do

Marrakech *p26, maps p32 and p37*
Ballooning
Ciel d'Afrique, Imm Ali, Apt 4, 2nd floor, Av Youssef Ben Tachfine, Route de Targa, Guéliz, T0524-432843, www.cieldafrique. info. An early morning hot air balloon flight over the palm groves and villages to the north of Marrakech is a great way to start the day. Starts from 2050dh per person. They also organize balloon trips further afield in the south of the country.

Climbing and outdoor activities
Terres d'Amanar, 35 km Rte de Asni (30 mins from Marrakech), T0524-438103, www.terresdamanar.com. In the foothills of Mt Toubkal National Park is a new eco-adventure forest park offering professionally supervized outdoor pursuits. Day courses include climbing, abseiling, zip wire, trekking and archery. There's also accommodation in eco-lodge or tents for longer stays.

Golf
Palmeraie Golf Palace Circuit de la Palmeraie, T0524-368766, www. pgp marrakech.com/golf/golf.html. 18-hole, and additional 9-hole course, designed by Robert Trent opened in 2009. Fee 500dh, 7 km north of town in Palmeraie at **Hotel Palmeraie Golf Palace**.
Royal Golf Club, 7 km south, off the Ouarzazate road (N9), T0524-409828, www.royalgolfmarrakech.com. Three 9-hole interconnected courses set in orchards, fee per 18-hole round 550dh including clubs, obligatory caddie 100dh, open daily.

Hammams
The Islamic requirement for ablutions and the lack of bathrooms in many Moroccan homes mean that the city's hammams are well used. They cost around 10dh per

A day by the pool

While many of Marrakech's riads have plunge pools, these are often not much bigger than a large bath. And with the coast a long way away for a day trip, out-of-town pools, usually with attached bars and restaurants, or hotels that open their pools to non-residents, can make an attractive day out, especially as the temperature rises in summer.

Beldi Country Club, Km 6, Rte du Barrage, T0524-383950, www.beldicountryclub. com. For a tranquil afternoon lounging by the pool after a delicious three-course lunch on the terrace, this is the perfect spot. 350dh including lunch, 250dh

children. Ring to reserve.

La Plage Rouge, T0524-378086, www. laplagerougemarrakech.com. 3000 sq m of swimming pool makes La Plage Rouge stand out from its competitors. There's sand too and a DJ at night. Waterside beds encourage lounging. Pricey restaurant and bar on site. 250dh entry, 125dh for kids, free shuttle.

Oasiria, T0524-380438, www.oasiria.com. Not just a pool, Oasiria is a large water park, with two pools, a river, huge water slides and a pirate ship. Café-restaurants in acres of gardens. Free shuttle from the city centre, 190dh, 110dh children.

person and are either single sex or have set hours or days for men and women. Massage and black soap scrubs cost extra but are not expensive. Remember to keep your knickers or shorts on in the hammam and take a spare dry pair with you.

Try one of those on Riad Zitoun el Kedim or **Hammam Dar el Bacha**, Rue Fatima Zohra. This is a large hammam dating from the early 1930s. The vestibule has a huge dome, and inside are 3 parallel marble-floored rooms, the last with underfloor heating.

Many riads have private hammams, though these offer a different sort of experience compared to the real thing. Riad staff may be happy to accompany you to apply soap and scrub you with a coarse exfoliating mitten. Other deluxe hammams in the medina offer beauty treatments and massages; expect to pay anything from 300dh for a hammam, scrub and massage with argan oil.

Horse riding

Cavaliers de l'Atlas, Rte de Casablanca (opposite Afriquia Station), Palmeraie, T0672-845579, www.lescavaliersdelatlas. com. Riding in the palm groves outside Marrakech or longer treks for several days. Novices and experienced riders catered for.

Trekking and tour operators

Atlas Sahara Trek, 6 bis Rue Houdhoud, Quartier Majorelle, T0524-313901, www. atlas-sahara-trek.com. One of the best trekking agencies in Marrakech, with 20 years' experience. Moroccan-born founder Bernard Fabry knows his deserts well.

Mountain Safari Tours, 64 Lot Laksour, Route de Casa, Guéliz, T0524-308777, www.mountainsafaritours.com. Specialist travel agency with 20 years of experience.

Mountain Voyage, Immeuble El Batoul, 2nd Floor, 5 Av Mohammed V, Guéliz, T0524-421996, www.mountain-voyage. com. Organized and recommended tour operator with English-speaking staff running upmarket treks in the Toubkal area and beyond (5-14 days). Owners of the luxurious **Kasbah du Toubkal** mountain hotel (see page 94).

Omni Tours, 220 Av Mohammed V, T0524-421660, www.omni-tours.com. Organizes 4WD vehicles, minibuses and coach hire. Also runs a range of day excursions and trips countrywide including desert and trekking tours.

SheherazadVentures, 55 Residence Ali, Av Mohammed VI, Guéliz, T0615-647918, www.sheherazadventures.com. English-

Moroccan company specializing in tailor-made desert tours. Special interest trips include pottery making, photography, volunteering and date picking.

⊖ Transport

Marrakech *p26, maps p32 and p37*
Air

Airport **Marrakech Menara** is clearly signposted from the centre. There are direct flights from London and other European cities. **EasyJet** (www.easyjet.com), **Ryanair** (www.ryanair.com) and **Royal Air Maroc** (www.royalairmaroc.com) all fly daily to **London**. There are also flights to **Manchester**, **Bristol**, **Nottingham** and **Edinburgh**. British Airways (www.british airways.com) have 3 flights per week to London. Other destinations include **Casablanca** (2 a day), as well as **Milan**, **Lyon**, **Brussels** (Fri), **Geneva**, **Oslo** and **Copenhagen**. There are daily flights to **Paris** and **Madrid**.

Airline offices Royal Air Maroc, 197 Av Mohammed V, T0890-00080 (call centre). Open 0830-1215 and 1430-1900.

Bus

Local city buses, run by **AlsaCity**, can be caught at the Pl de Foucault, just off Jemaâ el Fna next to the calèches. Stops are elsewhere along Av Mohammed V and Av Hassan II. No 1 and No 7 are the most useful, running from Jemaâ el Fna along Av Mohammed V, through Guéliz. No 3 and No 8 run from the railway station to the bus station, via Jemaâ el Fna; No 10 from Jemaâ el Fna to the bus station; No 11 from Jemaâ el Fna to the Menara Gardens and airport. No 4 goes to the Jardin Majorelle.

For long-distance journeys, the *gare routière* is just outside Bab Doukkala, T0524-433933, which is easily reached by taxis and local buses. There is often a choice between different companies with varying prices and times. When leaving Marrakech, make sure the number of the booth where the tickets are bought matches the bus stop number where you intend to catch the bus. Always be there in advance. It is wise to call at the station the previous day as some services, notably across the High Atlas to Taroudant and Ouarzazate, leave early in the morning. **CTM** (T0524-448328, www.ctm. ma) departures can also be caught from their terminal at Rue Abou Bakr Seddiq, near the Theatre Royal in Guéliz. **Supratours** (T0524-435525, www.supratours.ma) buses leave from alongside the train station on Av Hassan II, but can be full with pre-booked train travellers. Destinations include **Agadir**, **Casablanca**, **El Jadida**, **Er Rachidia**, **Essaouira** (best with Supratours), **Laâyoune**, **M'hamid** (CTM only), **Oualidia**, **Ouarzazate**, **Rabat**, **Safi**, **Skoura** and **Taroudant**.

Buses to the **Ourika Valley**, **Asni** and **Moulay Brahim** run from Bab Rob.

Calèche

Green-painted horse-drawn carriages can be hailed along Av Mohammed V or from the stands at Jemaâ el Fna and Pl de la Liberté. There are fixed prices for tours around the ramparts, other routes are up for negotiation, but they are not normally prohibitively expensive, and this is a pleasant way to see the city. Expect to pay around 150-200dh per hour. Some carriages have set prices displayed inside.

Car hire

You should be able to get something like a small Dacia or Renault Clio for 350dh per day, unlimited kilometres, but avoid the lesser-known firms, if possible, and make sure there's cover, or at the very least a plan B, in case you break down in the middle of nowhere. A driver will cost you around 250dh a day extra. 4WD hire with driver is around 1200dh per day. If driving, once out of Marrakech, the roads are rarely crowded. However, the Marrakech–Casablanca road has a notoriously high number of accidents. **Avis**, 137 Av Mohammed V, T0524-433727. **Europcar**, 63 Blvd Mohammed Zerktouni,

T0524-431228, and at the airport. **Hertz**, 154 Av Mohammed V, T0524-431394, airport T0524-447230.

Taxi

Petits taxis The city's khaki-coloured *petits taxis* are much in evidence and can take up to 3 passengers. As you get in, check the driver switches the meter on. Be firm but polite about not paying over the odds. From the medina to Guéliz should cost around 10dh during the day, 10-20dh after 2000. Taxis will try and overcharge to the airport; it's worth insisting on them using the meter or agreeing a price first. Major ranks are to be found in Jemaâ el Fna and at the *gare routière* by Bab Doukkala.

Grands taxis These can be found at the railway station and the major hotels. They also run over fixed routes, mainly to the suburbs, from Jemaâ el Fna and Bab Doukkala. They are cheap and convenient for visiting outlying areas and connecting to other cities, such as **Fès** (8 hrs). Prices vary depending on route. 6 passengers are normally squeezed in, but you can make a private trip if you pay for the empty spaces.

For the **Ourika Valley** and **Ouirgane**, they leave from Bab Rob. For **Asni** and **Imlil**, they leave from Av Mohammed VI, near **Pacha** (get a *petit taxi* to take you there). For most other destinations, including **Essaouira** and **Agadir**, go to Bab Doukkala. For destinations east, check out Bab Doukkala or Bab el Khemis.

Train

The railway station is in Guéliz, on Av Hassan II at the corner with Av Mohammed V, T0890-203040 (call centre), www.oncf.ma. Although there are plans for an eventual extension of the line south to Agadir and Laâyoune, at present ONCF operates only bus services to the south, connecting with the arrival of the express trains. There are express trains for **Casablanca** (3½ hrs), **Rabat** (4 hrs) and **Fès** (7 hrs).

Directory

Marrakech *p26, maps p32 and p37*
Banks The main concentrations of ATMs are on Rue Bab Agnaou (now called Av Prince Moulay Rachid) near the Pl Jemaâ el Fna, and in Guéliz on Av Mohammed V between Pl du 16 Novembre and the roundabout Abd el Moumen. If stuck at weekends and public holidays, then the **BMCI**, almost opposite the Cinéma Colisée on Blvd Zerktouni, is open 0930-1130 and 1600-1900. Otherwise, Mon-Fri 0900-1300 and 1500-1900.

Medical services Chemists: Pharmacie Centrale, 166 Av Mohammed V, T0524-430151. **Pharmacie de Paris**, 120 Av Mohammed V, T0524-447663. The préfecture operates an all-night pharmacy, the **Dépôt de nuit**, which looks like a ticket window on Pl Jemaâ el Fna (with the Koutoubia behind you, turn left after the stone wall of the Club Med compound). You may have to queue for some time. There is also an all-night chemist, **Pharmacie de Nuit**, at Rue Khalid Ben Oualid, Guéliz, T0524-430415 (doctor sometimes available). **Dentists**: Dr Hamid Laraqui, 203 Av Mohammed V, Guéliz, T0524-433216; Dr Gailleres, 112 Av Mohammed V, Guéliz, T0524-449136; Dr Karim Zihri, 117 Rue Mohammed Bequal, Apt 2, Guéliz, T0524-439030. All speak English. **Doctor on call**: T0524-404040 (ambulance service too), SAMU T0524-433030. **Doctors**: Dr Ahmed Mansouri, Clinique Ibn Rochd, Rue de Sebou, T0524-433079, and Dr G Michaelis Agoumi, 7 Rue Ibn Sina, Quatrier de l'Hopital Civile, Guéliz, T0524-448343. Both speak English. **Private hospital**: Polyclinique du Sud, 2 Rue de Yougoslavie, T0524-447999. **Polyclinique Les Narcisses**, Camp el Ghoul, 112 Route de Targa, T0524-447575.

Useful addresses Emergency services Private ambulance service: 10 Rue Fatima Zohra, T0524-443724. **Fire**: Rue Khalid Ben Oualid, T150. **Police**: Rue Ibn Hanbal, T190.

Essaouira

Essaouira, 'little picture', is one of those stage set places: you half expect to see plumed cavalry coming round the corner, or a camera crew filming some diva up on the ramparts. It is a beautifully designed 18th-century military port and, somehow, hasn't changed too much since. The walls are white, the windows and shutters are often cracked and faded blue, while arches and columns are sandy camel-brown. Three crescent moons on a city gate provide a touch of the heraldic, while surfers and fanciful Jimi Hendrix myths hint at Essaouira's hippy days, a few decades ago. (Though stories linking the ruins of Borj el Baroud with Hendrix's 'Castles Made of Sand' are spurious – the song was released 18 months before the singer visited Essaouira.) Tall feathery araucaria trees and palms along the ramparts add a Mediterranean touch. New flights to the airport may further reduce Essaouira's isolation, though currently most visitors still arrive by bus or taxi from Marrakech. Large numbers of foreigners have bought picturesque property and there are two successful music festivals.

Arriving in Essaouira

Getting there
Both **CTM** (www.ctm.ma) and private lines arrive at the bus station about 300 m northeast of the medina at Bab Doukkala – a five-minute walk with luggage or a 10dh *petit taxi* ride (15dh at night). *Grands taxis* also run to the bus station, although arrivals will be dropped off right next to the main entrance to the medina, Bab Doukkala. Drivers may want to use the car park (24-hour warden) close to the harbour next to Place Prince Moulay el Hassan.
▸▸ *See Transport, page 80, for further details.*

Getting around
One of the most appealing aspects of Essaouira is that all the principal tourist sites can be comfortably reached on foot; cars can be left in the car park. There are some good walks along the windswept beach to Borj el Beroud. The walk to Cap Sim is an all-day excursion.

Tourist information Délégation Provincial de Tourisme ① *10 Av du Caire, T0524-783532, Mon-Fri 0900-1630.* Rather basic office with helpful staff, maps, leaflets and bus timetables.

Background

Essaouira is a quiet sort of place with a long history. There was a small Phoenician settlement here, previously called Magdoura or Mogador, a corruption of the Berber word Amegdul, meaning 'well-protected'. The Romans were interested in the purple dye produced from the abundant shellfish on the rocky coast, which they used to colour the robes of the rich. Mogador was occupied in the 15th century by the Portuguese, who built the fortifications around the harbour. The town was one of their three most important bases, but was abandoned in 1541, from which time it went into decline. Mogador was also visited by Sir Francis Drake in Christmas 1577. In 1765, the Alaouite Sultan Sidi Mohammed Ibn Abdallah transformed Mogador into an open city, enticing overseas businessmen in with trade concessions, and it soon became a major commercial port, with a large foreign and Jewish population establishing the town as a major trading centre.

The sultan employed the French architect Théodore Cornut to design the city and its fortifications. In his design, Cornut chose a rectangular layout for the main streets, resulting in a uniform style, and constructed ramparts in the Vauban style. The fortifications were not always that effective, however. From time to time, the tribesmen of the region would raid the town, carrying off booty and the merchants' wives – who it is said, were not always that happy to return. Perhaps life in rural Morocco was more pleasant than listening to the wind in the damp counting houses of Mogador.

Orson Welles stayed here for some time, filming part of *Othello* at the Skala du Port. At Independence the town's official name became Essaouira, the local Arabic name meaning 'little picture'. In the 1960s Essaouira had a brief reputation as a happening place, attracting hippies and rockstars, including Jimi Hendrix.

Now the town is emerging from several decades of decline, for on top of fishing, fish processing, a small market and handicraft industries, the town is attracting greater numbers of tourists, notably surfers. The burgeoning number of riads and their accompanying upmarket tourism has also brought some wealth to the inhabitants of this most relaxed town, without spoiling its gentle atmosphere, though an increase in the number of oversized hotels outside the city walls may have a more detrimental effect.

Essaouira has some useful friends in influential places, including André Azoulay, one of HM the King's special advisers, and there is an artistic lobby, too, including gallery owner Frédéric Damgaard and Edmond Amran-Mellah, the writer. Dar Souiri, on Avenue de Caire opposite the Délégation de Tourisme, is the hub of the town's cultural activities.

Places in Essaouira → *For listings, see pages 74-81.*

Medina

Essaouira does not have a lot in the way of formal sights, but has plenty of gently atmospheric streets to compensate. Enclosed by walls with five main gates, the medina is the major attraction. Entering from **Bab Doukkala** the main thoroughfare is Rue Mohammed Zerktouni, which leads into Avenue de l'Istiqlal, where there is the **Grand Mosque**, and just off, on Darb Laalouj, the **Ensemble Artisanal** and the **Museum of Sidi Mohammed Ibn Abdallah**, which houses the **Museum of Traditional Art and Heritage of Essaouira** ⓘ *T0524-475300, Wed-Mon 0830-1200 and 1430-1800, 10dh*. This house, once the home of a pasha, has a collection of weapons and handicrafts, such as woodwork and carpets, and also has an interesting ethnographic collection, including examples of stringed instruments beautifully decorated with marquetry and documents on Berber music.

Avenue de l'Istiqlal leads into Avenue Okba Ibn Nafi, on which is located the small **Galerie d'Art Damgaard**. At the end of the street a gate on the right leads into **Place Moulay Hassan**, the heart of the town's social life. The town's souks are mainly around the junction between Rue Mohammed Zerktouni and Rue Mohammed el Gorry, although

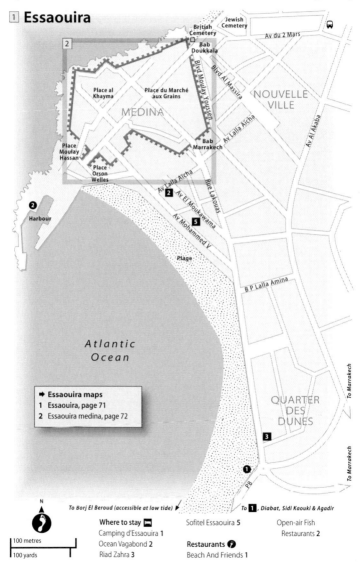

1 **Essaouira**

Jewish Cemetery

British Cemetery

Av du 2 Mars

Bab Doukkala

Blvd Moulay Youssef

Blvd Al Massira

2

Place al Khayma

Place du Marché aux Grains

NOUVELLE VILLE

MEDINA

Av Lalla Aïcha

Av Al Akaba

Place Moulay Hassan

Bab Marrakech

Place Orson Welles

Av Lalla Aïcha

2

Av El Moukaouama

Rue Lalouas

5

2 Harbour

Av Mohammed V

Plage

B P Lalla Amina

Atlantic Ocean

Essaouira maps
1 Essaouira, page 71
2 Essaouira medina, page 72

QUARTER DES DUNES

To Marrakech

3

To Marrakech

1

P B

N

100 metres

100 yards

To Borj El Beroud (accessible at low tide)

To **1**, Diabat, Sidi Kaouki & Agadir

To Marrakech

Where to stay 🛏
Camping d'Essaouira **1**
Ocean Vagabond **2**
Riad Zahra **3**

Sofitel Essaouira **5**

Restaurants 🍴
Beach And Friends **1**

Open-air Fish Restaurants **2**

there is an area of woodworkers inside the Skala walls to the north of Place Moulay Hassan, where some fine pieces can be picked up with some good-natured bargaining. At the northeast end of Rue Zerktouni, close to Bab Doukkala, is the much-decayed **mellah**, the old Jewish quarter. Although the Jewish community no longer remains, it made a substantial contribution to the commercial and cultural development of the town.

Outside Bab Doukkala is the Consul's **cemetery** for the British officials who died here while converting Mogador into a trading post with strong UK links. Behind the high wall on the road to the bus station is the **Jewish cemetery**. If you find the man with the key, you may discover the resting place of Leslie Hore-Belisha, inventor of the first pedestrian crossing light.

The Harbour and Skala du port

Off Place Moulay Hassan is the small harbour, busy with its fishing fleet. The open-air restaurant stalls serving grilled fish have been smartened up in recent years but are still a

☑ **Essaouira medina**

Where to stay 🛏
Beau Rivage **1**
Casa Lila **22**
Dar Liouba **21**
Dar Loulema **5**
Dar L'oussia **2**
Emeraude **8**
Essaouira Hostel **3**
La Maison des Artistes **4**
Lunetoile **18**
Riad Chakir **6**
Riad Lalla Mira **23**
Riad Le Grand Large **9**

Riad Nakhla **24**
Riad Watier **19**
Sahara **15**
Souiri **25**
Tea House **7**
Villa Garance **10**
Villa Maroc **17**

Restaurants 🍴
After 5 **12**
Café des Arts **10**
Café L'Opera **2**
Dar Al Houma **3**

Elizir **4**
El Minzah **13**
Ferdaouss **9**
Laayoune **5**
La Cantina **6**
La Découverte **11**
La Triskalla **8**
Le Patio **14**
Les Alizés **15**
Riad Al-Baraka **16**

great spot for lunch. The sea gate (**Porte de la Marine**), which serves to link the harbour with the medina, was built in 1769, it is said, by an Englishman who converted to Islam during the reign of Sidi Mohammed Ibn Abdallah. The gateway is built of stone in the classical style and the year of its construction (1184 of the Hegira) is inscribed on the pediment. It is connected to the ramparts on the **Skala**, an old Portuguese sea defence and battery, by a bridge which spans small primitive dry docks. Entry to the **Skala du Port** (10dh) is via a kiosk close to the Porte de la Marine, and from the top of the bastion there are extensive panoramic views of the harbour and the offshore islands, the **Îles Purpuraires**.

Skala de la Ville
Further to the north of Place Moulay Hassan, it is possible to get onto the ramparts of the Skala de la Ville from Rue de la Skala close to its junction with Rue Darb Laalouj. Entry here is free, and crenellated walls protect a 200-m-long raised artillery platform and an impressive array of decorated Spanish and other European cannon. This is a good spot from which to watch the sunset. From the tower of the **North Bastion** there are fine views of the old mellah, the medina, with its white buildings and blue shutters, and the coastline to the north. The **woodworkers' souks** are situated here in arched chambers underneath the ramparts.

Beaches
Essaouira has fine beaches. The prevailing wind, known as the *alizée*, stirs up a lot of sand and makes it cold for swimming, but ideal for windsurfing, though not necessarily surfing. The northern **Plage de Safi** is fine in the summer, but can be dangerous during windy weather. South of the town, the wide beach is great for football, and there are usually games going on here. Past the Oued Ksob, you will see the waves breaking against the remains of Borj el Baroud, an old fortress. When walking far along the beach it should be noted that the incoming tide makes the Oued Ksob below the village of Diabat into an impassable river.

Diabat
The one-time favourite hippy destination of Diabat, about 5 km from Essaouira, is easily reached by *petit* and *grand taxi*, say 40dh. The ruined palace/pavilion below Diabat is worth a visit. The building is said to have been swallowed by the sand after the people of the Souss put a curse on it because their trade was being ruined. The old fort was built by the Portuguese in the 18th century. A short walk up the road from Diabat will bring you to the **Auberge Tangaro**, one of Essaouira's better known hotels; 500 m further on, and you are at the crossroads with the N1 road from the south, which runs back into town.

Îles Purpuraires
These islands to the southwest are a bird sanctuary, particularly for rare Eleonora's falcons. With a good telescope it's possible to see these falcons from the end of the jetty. Another area frequented by the birds is the mouth of **Oued Ksob**. The river mouth is also noted for a variety of migrating seabirds, including black, little, sandwich, whiskered and white-winged terns. The *oued* can be reached from a track off the N1 south of the town but access to the sea is not easy. Although now a nature reserve, it is possible to visit the main island, **Île de Mogador**, outside the breeding season (it's closed April to October). You can negotiate a private trip with a local fishing vessel to ferry you there and back, but first must obtain a permit (free) from the Port office.

For hotel and restaurant price codes and other relevant information, see pages 10-16.

🛏 Where to stay

Essaouira *p69, maps p71 and p72*
The best place to stay is the medina, with its upmarket guesthouses, riads and occasionally damp cheap hotels. It's also possible to stay south of the medina, with a few large hotels and guesthouses stretching along the beachfront as far as the main Marrakech road. Alternatively, head for a country guesthouse a few miles south in Diabat, Ghazoua or Cap Sim.

When searching for cheap hotels make sure you get a well-ventilated room with windows and, preferably, a view of the ocean.

Riads and guesthouses
Essaouira is second only to Marrakech in the quantity and quality of restored properties in the old town operating as guesthouses. Though many of these are not riads in the strictest sense, they are usually referred to as such and the style will be familiar to those who have stayed in riads in Marrakech. If you can afford it, these are the best option. The typical Essaouira house has two storeys around a courtyard with rooms opening onto balconies.

Most guesthouses can do evening meals for around 150-200dh, if given advance warning. In many cases, the whole establishment can be rented for a few days for a house party. It is important to book well ahead, especially during the annual **Gnaoua Festival**. Many guesthouses do not accept credit cards; check in advance.

For a selection of apartments and riads, try agency **Jack's Kiosk**, 1 Pl Moulay Hassan, T0524-475538, www.jackapartments.com, or **Karimo**, T0524-474500, www.karimo.net.
€€€ Casa Lila, 94 Rue Mohammed el Qorry, T0524-475545, www.casalila-riad. com. Exceptionally photogenic, even by

riad standards, **Casa Lila** goes big on dusty pastel shades, with lots of purples and lilacs. Rooms come in different colour schemes but all are pretty; the fabrics are luscious, beds are sprinkled with petals, and open fires, floorboards and checkered floors add to the chic quotient. Stunning roof terrace. Minimum 2-night stay.
€€€ Dar Liouba, 28 Impasse Moulay Ismaïl, T0524-476297, www.darliouba.eu. Homely and French, this is a tall, thin guesthouse with rooms around an octagonal courtyard. The decoration is bright and simple with white walls and splashes of colour, though rooms are rather small. Rustic charm and some rooms with open fireplace. Family suites available. A very warm welcome. Heated in winter.
€€€ Dar Loulema, 2 Rue Souss, T0524-475346, www.darloulema.com. Centrally situated next to the **Café Taros**, this place has 8 beautifully styled rooms each with a/c and power shower. There's a pleasing mix of antique furnishings, traditional tiled floors and colourful fabrics. Very comfortable. Great views of the fishing port.
€€€ Riad Watier, 16 Rue Ceuta, T0524-476204, www.ryad-watier-maroc.com. The French owner of this large and spacious riad has filled it with stunning artworks by local painters, aboriginal artists and his own father. The huge rooms are each individually designed and some have mezzanine sleeping platforms. There's a cosy library full of interesting books, a resident tortoise and an air of relaxed charm. White walls add to the sense of light and there are tiles, rugs, terracotta *tadelakt* and big showers in all 10 rooms. Also a hammam and massage room. Meals upon request. Minimum 2-night stay.
€€€ Villa Garance, 10 Rue Eddakhil, T0524-473995, www.essaouira-garance. com. Well looked after by its French owners, **Villa Garance** has a pretty roof terrace with views over the sea and a

plant-draped central courtyard, with an open fireplace for winter. Bright rooms have decorative tiled floors, some have 4-poster beds and all have external windows on a quiet street. A playroom, babysitting service and 4-bedroom suite make it a good option for families.

€€€-€€ **La Maison des Artistes**, 19 Rue Laâlouj, T0524-475799, www.lamaison desartistes.com. There's an entertaining air of artistic eccentricity at this 7-room guesthouse overlooking the sea, with lots of conversation point pieces of furniture and striking art among the colourful decoration. 'Le Pavilion de Cesar' has stunning wrap-around sea views, as does the roof terrace. An enticing menu of home-made meals prepared upon request. Breakfast and soft drinks included.

€€€-€€ **Riad Lalla Mira**, 14 Rue d'Algerie, T0524-475046, www.lallamira.net. German-run **Lalla Mira** emphasizes its eco-credentials and also houses a beautiful mosaic-tiled hammam (the oldest in Essaouira), free for guests. The 10 en suite rooms have solar-powered underfloor heating, water-recycling system and hypoallergenic mattresses, draped with organic cotton. Restaurant serves good vegetarian food. Price includes breakfast.

€€€-€€ **The Tea House**, 74 Derb Laalouj, La Skala, T0524-783543, www.theteahouse. net. Despite its English name, Alison MacDonald runs this small guesthouse very much in the traditional Essaouira vein. The 200-year-old house is beautifully decorated, with antiques and pale pastel-painted walls. The 1st and 2nd floors are available for rent, each apartment accommodating up to 4, with kitchen, sitting room, open fire, 2 bedrooms and large bathroom. Shared roof terrace, breakfast and firewood are included. Price is £32 per person, 3rd and 4th guests are half price. Solo travelers can rent apartment for £45. Price calculated in local currency at time of booking.

€€ **Lunetoile**, 191 Rue Sidi Mohammed Ben Abdullah, T0524-474689, www.lunetoile riad.com. Low key and good value, **Lunetoile** is off the beaten track in the mellah, and you'll probably be able to hear the sea and the seagulls from your room. In places the blue and yellow colour scheme is a little jarring but it has a genuine Moroccan feel, it's homely and the large apartments are a great option for families. Up to half price Jan-Mar.

€€ **Riad Chakir**, Rue Malek Ben Morhal (off Av Istiqlal), T0524-473309, www. riadchakir.com. Loads of traditional Moroccan character in these 2 adjoining houses, which offer 20 rooms around stone-columned patios, with colourful painted ceilings, chunky wooden beams and en suite *tadelakt* bathrooms. Some of the rooms are very cramped, but service is friendly and it's very affordable. Central location, close to car park.

€€ **Riad Le Grand Large**, 2 Rue Oum-Rabia, T0524-472866, www. riadlegrandlarge.com. The name is not only tautological, it's not really true, but this is a good, colourful, and good-value option, with 10 cheerful and unfussy en suite rooms, heated in winter, the best of which overlook the street. There's a roof terrace and a restaurant.

€ **Essaouira Hostel**, 17 Rue Laghrissi, T0524-476481, essaouirahostel@gmail. com. Tricky to find, but ring ahead and somebody will come to meet you. A 'boutique' hostel in an 18th-century riad with superb friendly management and youthful vibe. Private rooms and dorms available. Winner of 2nd prize in Hoscar Awards for best hostels in Africa 2008. Dorm from 90dh. Breakfast 20dh or make your own meals in the communal kitchen.

Hotels

€€€ **Hotel Dar l'Oussia**, 4 Rue Mohammed Ben Messaoud, T05234-783756, www.dar loussia.com. A large place for the medina, this offers 20 spacious rooms and 4 suites around a central courtyard. Rooms are stylishly decorated with traditional tiling and fabrics in pale colours. Underfloor heating, free Wi-Fi, free hammam, spa, restaurant and bar.

€€€ Hotel Villa Maroc, 10 Rue Abdallah Ben Yassin, T0524-476147, www.villa-maroc.com. Converted from 4 merchants' houses, this was one of the first boutique hotels in Morocco. Beautifully decorated around a central court festooned with plants and greenery, roof terrace with superb views. There are 17 rooms, and an apartment sleeping 4 is available. Restaurant with great food, hammam and spa treatments, free Wi-Fi. Book ahead.

€€ Hotel Emeraude, 228 Rue Chebanate, near the little gate of Bab Marrakech, T0524-473494, www.essaouirahotel.com. Small, attractive Franco-Moroccan-run hotel on the dry side of the medina. One of best small hotels in town, with 8 attractive doubles and 2 triples. Stylish and convenient, with guarded car parking just 40 m away.

€ Hotel Beau Rivage, Pl Moulay Hassan, T0524-475925, www.beaurivage-essaouira.com. Some of the 21 rooms in this central hotel have balconies overlooking the main square, others have a sea view. The decor is dated and worn out, but it's clean and has friendly, helpful management and a roof terrace. Breakfast is 20dh.

€ Hotel Cap Sim, 11 Rue Ibn Rochd, T0524-785834. Clean and cheap, just round the corner from Pl Moulay Hassan and a patisserie opposite, which gets noisy at night. Simple rooms with comfy beds, very clean with tiles, coloured glass and a central courtyard. Not all rooms have bathroom. Price includes breakfast.

€ Hotel Riad Nakhla, 12 Rue d'Agadir, T0524-474940, www.essaouiranet.com/riad-nakhla. 18 rooms, all with private bathrooms (though some rather shabby), for a budget price and in a convenient location. The decoration may not be quite up to the level of its riad competitors but there's a courtyard with a fountain and a roof terrace for breakfast. It's attractive, comfortable and has helpful staff. Very good value.

€ Hotel Sahara, Av Okba Ibn Nafi, T0524-475292, www.hotelsahara-essaouira.com. Comfortable and central, Sahara has a range of rooms (70), some of which are fine and functional. Cheaper rooms opening onto the inner courtyard are darker, less well ventilated and can be noisy.

€ Hotel Souiri, 37 Rue Attarine, T0524-475339, www.hotelsouiri.com. A fairly modern hotel, Souiri has 36 bright, clean rooms over 3 floors and a 2-room rooftop apartment ideal for families. It's decorated in a quasi-European style, and all rooms have TV. Category 1 rooms have nicer furniture and en suite bathrooms. There's a roof terrace with sun loungers.

Outside the medina

Outside the medina, most of Essaouira's hotels are big and too characterless to recommend, though there are a few seafront options worth considering if being near the beach is important.

€€€ Ocean Vagabond, 4 Blvd Lalla Aïcha, Angle Rue Moukawama, T0524-479222, www.hoteloceanvagabondessaouira.com. Facing the beach, but only around 200 m from the medina, the **Ocean Vagabond** lacks some of the atmosphere of a medina riad, but is attractively decorated with African-themed bar, library, cosy lounge and gardens with pool. The 14 rooms have marble and *tadelakt* bathrooms, sea-view balconies and plenty of mod cons.

€€€ Sofitel Essaouira Medina & Spa, Av Mohammed V, T0524-479000, www.sofitel.com. Opposite the beach, this is a large and luxurious 5-star hotel, with 117 rooms decorated in a contemporary version of traditional Moroccan style. Big heated pool and sheltered terraces, with palms and a good bar and restaurant. Luxurious spa and access to newly opened **Mogador Golf** course a few kilometres out of town. Multi-night deals often available online.

€€€-€€ Riad Zahra, 90 Quartier des Dunes, T0524-474822, www.riadzahra.com. Spanish-run small family hotel just off the seafront at the very southern end of the beach. 23 spacious rooms around an airy courtyard, with hand-painted furniture and Berber throws. All en suite and some have balconies or sea view. Restaurant and bar, terrace with fab ocean views, good-sized pool (shared with resident turtles), parking. 20 mins' walk to medina. It's more for a sea view.

Outside Essaouira

€€€ Baoussala, El Ghazoua, T0524-792345, www.baoussala.com. A small, pretty eco-guesthouse with a solar-heated pool, surrounded by terrace and gardens. 6 very tastefully designed en suite rooms in a peaceful location 10 km from Essaouira and 10 km from Sidi Kaouki. Purpose-built by owners Dominique and Bruno Maté in extensive grounds. Whole house can be rented. Lunch and evening meals available.

€€€ Jardins des Douars, Douar Sidi Yassine (15 km south of Essaouria, 3 km inland off the road to Agadir), T0524-474003, www.jardindesdouars.com. You'll need your own transport to find this delightful hideaway, but well worth the detour. Walls of warm *tadelakt*, hude wooden doors, fireplace and antique furniture. Tranquil surroundings with botanical gardens, spa and 2 pools. Split-level rooms, suites or private *douars* plus a restaurant and bar make this ideal for families.

€€ Auberge de la Plage, Sidi Kaouki, T0524-476600, www.kaouki.com. A colourful, chilled place. 10 bright rooms (2 with shared bathroom). Recently renovated and now full electricity supply, solar-heated hot water and intermittent Wi-Fi. Lovely shaded gardens. Horse riding and camel excursions.

€€ Dar Kenavo, 13 km out of Essaouira on Agadir road, after 8 km take the left turn for Casablanca/Marrakech and it's 4 km along on the left, T0661-207069 (mob), www.dar kenavo.com. Out in argan country, a small house with a heated pool and 7 rooms, 2 suites and a private bungalow around

a pleasant patio. A quiet corner to see something of Moroccan rural life. There's also a Berber tent. Disabled access.

€€ Hotel Villa Soleil, Plage de Sidi Kaouki, about 20 km south of Essaouira (the turn-off for Sidi Kaouki is some 15 km south of Essaouira on the Agadir road), T0524-472092, www.hotelvillasoleil.com. 9 simple rooms and a penthouse apartment arranged around a courtyard. All rooms en suite and with private terrace, shaded by palm trees and conifers. Right on the beach, no pool.

€€ Résidence Le Kaouki, 15 km south of Essaouira on road to Agadir, T0524-783206, www.sidikaouki.com. 10 simple rooms and a candlelit restaurant with an open fire. Ideal for windsurfers, 200 m from the beach. Can also arrange other activities and excursions.

Camping

Camping d'Essaouira, 2 km out of Essaouira near the lighthouse, on the Agadir road. Well protected, clean loos.

Restaurants

Essaouira *p69, maps p71 and p72*

€€€ After 5, 7 Rue Youssef el Fassi, T0524-473349. Open daily for lunch and dinner. Formerly 'Le 5', After 5 is no longer under French management, but it's retained the imaginative European and Moroccan menu. There's a 'super brunch' or modern dishes, such as carpaccio of swordfish with ginger. The whole place is very chic and inviting, with striking design features, such as lightshades big enough to live in. There's also a *salon de thé* and Wi-Fi. Alcohol served.

€€ Les Alizés, 26 Rue de la Skala, T0524-476819. Open daily for lunch and dinner. One of the most popular places in town, and rightfully so. You can't reserve, but waiting at the small tables just inside the entrance with some olives and a bottle of wine is one of the great pleasures of the place. Once you get a table, you'll be plied with great

Moroccan food – there's not an enormous choice but it's all good, and the place is run with a rare combination of efficiency and good humour. Alcohol served.

€€ Elizir, 1 Rue d'Agadir, T0524-472103. Open daily for lunch and dinner. Creative food using top-notch ingredients, run by a Moroccan recently returned from Italy. In a short time it has gained the reputation as the best restaurant in town. Try the ravioli with ricotta, basil and pistachio, or organic chicken with figs and gorgonzola. Eclectic decor, quirky touches and well-chosen music. Alcohol served. Booking advisable.

€€ El Minzah, 3 Av Oqba Ibn Nafia, T0524-475308. Open daily for lunch and dinner. A restaurant and piano bar just inside the walls near the clocktower. Good seafood options, including blue shark. A mellow, sophisticated spot for a drink with live Gnawa music on Sat. Good-value Moroccan fixed menu, or splash out three times as much on the French one. Alcohol served.

€€ Le Patio, 28 Bis Rue Moulay Rachid, T0524-474166. Tue-Sun dinner only; closed Jul. Imaginative Moroccan cuisine with a little French influence in their combination of spices and fruit. It's a stylish and atmospheric place, with warm low lighting, arches and flickering candlelight. Alcohol served, try the rum punch.

€€ Riad Al-Baraka, 113 Rue Mohammed al Qorry (near Bab Marrakech), T0524-473561. Open daily for lunch and dinner. Courtyard restaurant in what was once a Jewish school. Shaded patio ideal for lunch on a sunny day, or on cooler evenings the restaurant has an open fire. Mostly Moroccan and French cuisine, with live music at weekends. Alcohol served.

€ Beach and Friends, Blvd Mohammed V (at southern end of the beach), T0524-474558. Daily lunch and dinner. Right on the shorefront in a modern wooden cabin, a relaxed café-restaurant with sun-drenched indoor or shaded outdoor seating, as well as sun-loungers on the sand. Serves huge salads, tagines, burgers, paninis, pizzas and light snacks. Great for kids. Alcohol served.

€ Dar Al Houma, 9 Rue el Hajjali, T0524-783387. Daily lunch and dinner. There's a rare vegetarian set menu (60dh) as well as more standard Moroccan menus at this cosy little place just inside the walls of the medina. Very good value. English spoken. No alcohol. Cash only.

€ Ferdaouss, 27 Rue Abdesslam Lebadi, T0524-473655. Mon-Sat lunch and dinner. A popular place for Moroccan home cooking, this place is family run and found in an upstairs apartment. The food is reliable and good value, with the usual selection of *pastillas*, couscous and tagines. Bring your own wine.

€ Fish stalls, by far the best cheap eating option is to sample the freshly caught fish, grilled at the open-air restaurants between Pl Moulay Hassan and the port; accompanied by a tomato salad this makes a meal at a reasonable price. The standard of hygiene is good. Prices are fixed by weight and displayed on boards, but make sure you are clear on what you have and haven't ordered. The sales pitch can be a bit aggressive as you try to work your way past the stallholders. A cheaper option is the little fish barbecue place in **Souk el Hout**, the fish market in the town centre (the one on the left as you come from the port area down Av Istikal). No alcohol. Cash only.

€ Laayoune, 4 Rue el Hajjadi, T0524-474643. Daily lunch and dinner. Traditional, small and reliable, **Laayoune**, just on the inside of the walls, has a cosy candlelit vibe and great-value fixed menus 60dh-80dh. No alcohol. Cash only.

€ Restaurant La Découverte, 8 Rue Houmman, T0524-473158, www.essaouira-ladecouverte.com. Sun-Fri lunch and dinner. A friendly little French-run place offering such delicacies as lentil salad with argan oil and vegetable gratin, as well as meatier Moroccan choices. Wi-Fi. No alcohol. Cash only.

Cafés and ice cream

The best places for breakfast are on Pl
Moulay Hassan, particularly **Café L'Opéra**
and **Chez Driss**, where it's better value
than a cheap hotel, and no one seems to
mind if you bring your own cakes. There
are beachside cafés, too.

Café des Arts, 56 Av Istikal, T0612-134742.
Upstairs on the main street, this place
has a young vibe, with live music, art
and Moroccan food. Good for a lunch
or a quick snack.

Café Taros, 2 Rue de la Skala, T0524-476407,
www.taroscafe.com. Mon-Sat till late. Up
the street on your left as you face Pl Moulay
Hassan with port behind you, this café has a
bar and good food. There are lots of books
and magazines in the café area. Fabulous
roof terrace with bar for sunset cocktails.

Gelateria Dolce Freddo, Pl Moulay Hassan.
Right on the main square, this café does a
roaring trade in delicious ice cream.

La Cantina, 66 Rue Boutouil, T0524-474515.
English-run Mexican bistro-café serving
burgers, chilli con carne, veggie food,
home-made breads, cakes and scones.
Also has book swap and local info. Located
in a small square near the mellah.

La Triskalla, 58 Rue Touahen, T0524-
476371. A very laid-back café with free
internet and Wi-Fi, low lighting, candles
and a cat. Plenty of veggie options, snacks
and pancakes dominate the menu, and
there's an extensive selection of juices,
some of which are a tad over-imaginative.

Entertainment

Essaouira *p69, maps p71 and p72*
Essaouira is not really the place for wild
nightlife, although it livens up nicely
during the annual **Gnaoua Music Festival**
in Jun. The roof terrace lounge bar of **Café
Taros** (see above) is usually the liveliest
spot after sundown. **El Minzah** (see
Restaurants) or the bar in the **Hotel Sofitel**
offer upmarket alternatives.

The main alcohol off-licence is near Bab
Doukkala. Turn right out of the gate and the
off-licence is on your left after about 100 m,
identifiable by small black-and-white tiles
and beer posters.

Festivals

Essaouira *p69, maps p71 and p72*
May Les Alizés (www.alizesfestival.com)
classical music festival.
End Jun Gnaoua Music Festival.

Shopping

Essaouira *p69, maps p71 and p72*
The main thoroughfares of the southern
and central medina are all packed with
little boutiques, from traditional jewellery
stores and carpet merchants to funky
modern designer shops and scrap-metal
sculpture studios. Objects made in fragrant,
honey-brown thuya wood are everywhere,
from small boxes inlaid with lemon-wood
to chunky, rounded sculptures. More
expensively, you can pick up paintings by
the local school of naïve and pointillist
artists. Traditionally, the town's women
wore all-enveloping cotton/wool mix
wraps, in cream or brown, just the thing to
keep out the ocean mists. Islamic fashions
change and, happily, the weavers have
found a new market providing fabrics for
maisons d'hôte and their denizens. New
colours and stripes have been added,
and you can get a nice bedspread for
300dh. In Essaouira, you can also find
plenty of flowing shirts and pantaloons
in psychedelic designs or African cotton
print. Raffia-work sandals and handbags
and colourful felt accessories are also 'à la
mode'. Essaouira is also the place to pick
up the much-prized argan oil used for
cosmetic and food products.

Argan d'Or, 5 Rue Ibn Rochd. Sells a range
of argan beauty products and soaps.

Co-operative Tiguemine Argan, 15 km
Rte de Marrakech, T0524-784970. Get

to understand the argan oil production process by visiting this women's co-operative 15 km out of town on the road to Marrakech. There are several other co-ops along this stretch of highway.

KifKif, Pl aux Grains. Locally made accessories, jewellery and knick-knacks with a contemporary edge.

Raffia Craft, 82 Rue d'Agadir. This is a tiny outlet shop for the raffia products of local designer, Miro. His shoes are in demand in Europe and much copied by other local artisans.

Tamounte Co-Operative, 6 Rue Souss (off Pl Moulay Hassan). Sells hand-crafted gifts and games made from thuya wood.

What to do

Essaouira *p69, maps p71 and p72*
Cycling
Bikes, including mountain bikes, can be hired in the old town and from the **Explora** kitesurf shop in the square off Rue Laalouj from €15 per day.

Hammams
There are several public hammams in the medina, with prices from around 10dh for entry (extra for glove, soap and scrub-down). Try the oldest called **Hammam Pabst** on Rue Annasr in the mellah. Orson Welles once used it as a location in the filming of *Othello*. Alternatively, try the more upmarket and very popular **Mounia Hammam**, 17 Rue Oum Errabia. Prices from 50dh for a basic hammam and up to 250dh for the full works.

Horse riding
Ranch de Diabat, Diabat, Quartier des Dunes, T0670-576841, www.ranchdediabat.com. A ranch just 3 km south of Essaouira towards Agadir where you can do short rides along the beach or multi-day treks. Also organizes camel treks.

Surfing
Winter is the surfing season in Essaouira. Apr-Oct the wind is up and the surfers are out in force. If you don't have your own gear, you can rent but check it carefully. The best surf places are probably:

Club Mistral, right on the main beach at southern end of Blvd Mohammed V, T0524-783934, www.club-mistral.com. Formerly **Ocean Vagabond** and a long-established professional watersports outfitter.

Explora, T0611-475188, www.exploramorocco.com. Next to **Club Mistral** on the main beach. English-speaking staff and good value. Surf lessons from 300dh for 2 hrs. You can buy your gear here too or in their shop in the medina (see under Cycling, above).

Walking
Ecotourism and Randonnées, T0615-762131, www.essaouira-randonnees.com. Half-day and day walks with a picnic through the thuya forest and countryside around Essaouira. Organized from the **Restaurant la Découverte** (see Restaurants). English guide available.

Transport

Essaouira *p69, maps p71 and p72*
Air
RAM run flights to **Paris** and **Casablanca** from the little Aéroport de Mogador, T0524-476709.

Bus
Buses from Essaouira can get very full in summer and during the **Gnaoua Festival** in Jun; see Festivals, above. Check your departure times the day before you travel and try to reserve.

CTM (T0524-784764, www.ctm.ma) and private line bus services operate from the terminal near Bab Doukkala, with connections to **Casablanca** (6 or 9 hrs, depending on route), **Safi**, **Marrakech** (3 hrs) and **Agadir** (3½ hrs). You can also buy CTM bus tickets from their office on Rue de Caire near Bab Sabaa. Lots of touts compete for custom – go inside the terminus and look at ticket windows where departure times are clearly posted. **CTM** has departures daily at 0745 and 1130 to **Safi**, **El Jadida** and **Casablanca**. Buses south to **Agadir** depart at 1430 (60dh), and twice daily for **Marrakech** at 1230 and 1700 (75dh).

The best onward option is the **Supratours** (Essaouira office, T0524-475317, www. supratours.ma) service to **Marrakech** at 0600, 0930, 1145, 1500 and 1800 (70dh) to connect with onward trains to **Casablanca–Rabat**, from the square near the South Bastion. Buy your ticket at the kiosk on the square at least a day before, as this is a popular bus. **Pullman du Sud** has a midnight departure from the bus station for **Casablanca**, arriving at 0630.

Taxi

Grands taxis operate from a parking lot beside the bus terminal. (You may have to wait a while for the vehicle to fill up if you are going to Marrakech.) There are frequent departures for **Diabat**, **Ghazoua**, **Smimou** and other places in the region, also for **Marrakech** and **Agadir**. *Petits taxis* are numerous; 5dh for a short ride in town. There are numerous calèches to be caught from the cab rank outside Bab Doukkala.

ⓘ Directory

Essaouira *p69, maps p71 and p72*
Banks Branches of BMCI, BMCE, Banque Populaire and Crédit du Maroc are in and around Pl Moulay Hassan, most with ATM machines. **Medical services** Dentist: Dr ElAcham, 1 Blvd de Fès, T0524-474727; Dr Sayegh, Pl de l'Horloge, T0524-475569. **Doctor**: Dr Mohammed Tadrart, 1 Av Mouqawama, opposite post office, T0524-475954; Dr Said El-Haddad, 5 Av de l'Istiqlal, close to the Wafa Bank, T0524-476910. **Hospital**: Hôpital Sidi Mohammed ben Abdallah, Blvd de l'Hôpital (Emergencies), T0524-475716. **Pharmacies**: Av de l'Istiqlal and on Pl de l'Horloge in medina. Several pharmacies on Av Al Massira near Bab Doukkala. **Useful numbers** Police: main commissariat on Rue du Caire, T0524-784880.

Contents

Footprint features

Western High Atlas

Three main roads lead south out of Marrakech into the Western High Atlas. From west to east, they head over the Tizi-n-Test pass towards Taroudant; up the Ourika Valley to Setti Fatma, Oukaïmeden and the Toubkal National Park, and over the Tizi-n-Tichka pass towards Ouarzazate.

On the R203 to the Tizi-n-Test, Asni is an important market town and Ouirgane is a strung-out holiday destination in the hills. Further south, the road curves and rises through the spectacular mountain valley to the awe-inspiring 12th-century mosque of Tin Mal, one of Morocco's most significant buildings, now partially restored. Back at Asni, a road branches south to Imlil and the Toubkal National Park, centring on North Africa's highest mountain. The landscapes are spectacular, and there are some great walking routes.

The route up the Ourika Valley from Marrakech is, initially at least, a gentler one, splitting to terminate at either the village of Setti Fatma, with its waterfalls and riverside restaurants, or the ski resort of Oukaïmeden.

Most switch-back of all, the N9 climbs to cross through the Tizi-n-Tichka pass at 2260 m. Just east of here is the precipitous Kasbah of Telouet.

Southwest of Marrakech → For listings, see pages 93-97.

Take the main S501 road south out of Marrakech (straight over at the junction near the **Hivernage**). The road forks a few kilometres after the **Club Royal Equestre**. You go left for Asni (S501; see page 85), right for Amizmiz in the foothills of the Atlas. The latter road (S507) passes through a number of small settlements, including Tamesloht, and the Lalla Takerkoust Lake, where accommodation is available. Note that in a wet year, clay from the hillside may crumble onto the upper sections of the Amizmiz to Ouirgane road.

Lalla Takerkoust
Often referred to as 'the lake', Lalla Takerkoust, 40 km to the southwest of Marrakech, is actually a reservoir, formed by a hydroelectric dam (the Barrage Lalla Takerkoust) that provides Marrakech with a good portion of its electricity. It is a popular swimming and picnicking place for Marrakchis wanting to escape the oppressive heat of the city. Lapping at the red-earth foothills of the High Atlas, and with the high peaks as a backdrop, it's a

Un stylo, un bonbon, un dirham

All over the country the sight of children begging is not uncommon. But in the mountains it seems particularly prevalent, spurred on perhaps by generations of well-meaning trekkers who have happily handed out coins, pens or sweets. The mechanical chorus of "Un stylo, un bonbon, un dirham" will follow you, echoing through many remote mountain valleys.

In the past, the advice has been to bring a supply of pens to hand out or, in some worrying cases, medicine. Talk to local community leaders now, though, and they will almost certainly advise against giving the local children anything at all. Even giving out pens encourages systematic begging, damaging the education system and family structures. It also detrimentally affects the way foreign visitors are seen: as resources to be mined, rather than human beings to interact with.

Talk to the local children, teach them something, but save your pen money and donate it instead to organizations like the **Global Diversity Foundation** (www.globaldiversity.org.uk) or the **High Atlas Foundation** (www.highatlasfoundation.org).

strikingly beautiful place, and there are a couple of places to stay and eat (see page 93) too. If you have a car, the route across the Kik plateau from here to Asni has extraordinary panoramic views across the high pastures to the Atlas peaks beyond.

Amizmiz

Amizmiz, 55 km southwest from Marrakech at the end of the S507, is a growing rural centre interesting as the starting point of some pleasant hikes and for its Tuesday souk.

Turning off right just after the 'administrative zone', you can wind up into the foothills to the *maison forestière*. Parking in the shade, there is some gentle walking along a track above the Assif Anougal, with views down over the villages. From Amizmiz, there is also a road eastwards to **Ouirgane**, via the Tizi-n-Ouzla (1090 m), where you can get a view of the Assif Amassine valley, with the Toubkal Massif as backdrop. There then follows a winding descent to the junction with the S501, where you can go right for Ouirgane or left for Asni and Marrakech.

Moulay Brahim

With small hotels and eateries, Moulay Brahim is a popular weekend stop for Marrakchis. The village gets particularly busy from June to September, with people coming to visit the shrine of Moulay Brahim, visible with its green-tiled pyramid roof in the middle of the village. Stalls selling various scraggy pelts, chameleons and incense are evidence of the various favours that may be asked of Moulay Brahim. He is said to be particularly good at solving women's fertility problems. There is a festive atmosphere, with whole families coming to rent small semi-furnished apartments.

Asni

After the rather nerve-racking drive through the gorges of Moulay Brahim, the approach to Asni, with its poplar and willow trees, comes as something of a relief. If you arrive on Saturday, you will be able to see the souk in a big dusty enclosure on your left as you come from Marrakech, with its accompanying chaos of *grands taxis*, mules and minibuses. The village is scattered in clusters in the valley and makes a good place for a quick break en route to Ouirgane, Tin Mal or Taroudant, if you can deal with the attentions of the trinket sellers. There are good walking routes along the Plateau du Kik to the west of Asni, north to Moulay Brahim and southwest to Ouirgane.

A popular driving route goes from Asni up onto the **Plateau du Kik** and then through the villages around Tiferouine, before heading some 8 km northwest cross-country to the settlement of **Lalla Takerkoust** and its reservoir lake (see page 84).

Ouirgane

Ouirgane is another pleasant place to pause on the R203, about one hour's drive (61 km) from Marrakech. The settlement's houses are scattered on the valley sides, and some have been recently displaced by the building of a new dam on the Oued Nfiss. Ouirgane can be reached by bus from Marrakech (the Taroudant service), or by *grands taxi* from Asni. Hotels in Ouirgane (see page 93) have good food and offer the opportunity to explore the valley on easy rambles.

Tin Mal

A small settlement high in the Atlas mountains, Tin Mal was once the holy city of the Almohad Dynasty. It offers a rare opportunity for non-Muslims to see the interior of a major Moroccan mosque, with examples of 12th-century Almohad decor intact amidst the ruins. The Koutoubia at Marrakech (the Almohad capital from 1147) was modelled on Tin Mal. At the mosque the guardian will let you in and point out enthusiastically features such as the original doors piled up in a corner. He'll also ask for a donation when you leave.

Background In 1122, Ibn Toumert, after much roaming in search of wisdom, returned to Morocco. He created too much trouble in Marrakech, with his criticisms of the effete Almoravids, and shortly after, when the mountain tribes had sworn to support him and fight the Almoravids in the name of the doctrines he had taught them, he was proclaimed Mahdi, the rightly guided one. In 1125 he established his capital at Tin Mal, a fairly anonymous hamlet strategically situated in the heartland of his tribal supporters. The rough-and-ready village was replaced with a walled town, soon to become the spiritual centre of an empire. The first mosque was a simple affair. The building you see today, a low square structure, was the work of Ibn Toumert's successor, Abd el Mu'min – a student whom the future Mahdi had met in Bejaïa.

Tin Mal was the first *ribat*, as the austere Almohad fortresses were called, and was subject to a puritan discipline. The Mahdi himself was a sober, chaste person, an enemy of luxurious living. All his efforts went into persuading his followers of the truths of Islam, as he conceived them. Tin Mal was subject to a pitiless discipline. Prayers were led by the Mahdi himself and all had to attend. Public whippings and the threat of execution kept those lacking in religious fervour in line. As well as prayer leader, the Mahdi was judge, hearing and trying cases himself according to Muslim law, which had barely begun to penetrate the mountain regions.

After Ibn Toumert's death, his simple tomb became the focal point for a mausoleum for the Almohad sovereigns. Standing in the quiet mosque, today mostly open to the sky, looking down the carefully restored perspectives of the arcades, it is difficult to imagine what a hive of religious enthusiasm this place must have been.

Tin Mal mosque Completed in 1154, under Abd el Mu'min, the Tin Mal Mosque has a simple exterior. The mihrab (prayer niche) is built into the minaret. To the left, as one stands before the mihrab, is the imam's entrance to the right is a space for the minbar, the preacher's chair, which would have been pulled out for sermons. The decoration is simple: there are several cupolas with restored areas of stalactite plasterwork and there are examples of the *darj w ktaf* and palmette motifs, but little inscription. The technique used, plaster applied to brick, is a forerunner of later, larger Almohad decorative schemes.

When the new empire acquired Marrakech, a fine capital well located on the plain, Tin Mal remained its spiritual heart and a sort of reliable rear base. It was to Tin Mal that Abd el Mu'min sent the treasures of Ibn Tachfin the Almoravid. Even after the Merinid destruction of 1275-1276, the tombs of of Ibn Toumert and his successors inspired deep respect.

Eventually, the Almohads were to collapse in internecine struggles. The final act came in the 1270s, when the last Almohads took refuge in Tin Mal. However, the governor of Marrakech, El Mohallim pursued them into their mountain fastness, and besieged and took the seemingly impenetrable town. The Almohad caliph and his followers were taken prisoner and executed, and the great Almohad sovereigns, Abu Yaqoub and Abu Youssef, were pulled from their tombs and decapitated. The Almohads, one time conquerors of the whole of the Maghreb and much of Spain, were destroyed in their very capital, barely 150 years after they had swept away the Almoravids.

In the 1990s, around US$750,000 was put forward for restoration of the ruins. Work now seems to have ground to a halt, though the building is doubly impressive in its semi-ruined, semi-open-to-the-sky way.

Tizi-n-Test

The R203 from Marrakech to Taroudant is one of the most spectacular routes in Morocco, winding its way up and then down through the High Atlas mountains, above beautiful valleys and past isolated villages, eventually reaching the Tizi-n-Test pass, with its breathtaking views across the Souss valley to the Anti-Atlas mountains. There are buses between the two cities, but check that they are going via Tizi-n-Test. Driving has been possible since the road, a traditional trading route, was formally opened in 1928, following the work of French engineers. Some of its sections are downright scary, but it is a recommended experience, particularly when tied in with visits to Asni, Ouirgane and Tin Mal. Signs on the exit to Marrakech will indicate if the pass is open. The R203 joins the N10 from Taroudant to Ouarzazate. For a lunch stop on this route, there is the cheap **Restaurant La Belle Vue**, about 1 km after the pass on the Taroudant side. Cheap rooms are also available, but have a sleeping bag ready – it gets cold at 2100 m altitude.

Imlil and the Toubkal National Park → *See also map, page 89.*

Northern Africa's highest peak is one that many like to tick off their list, but the national park that surrounds it has plenty of other good walks, from afternoon strolls to serious treks. For details of walks in the park see box, page 90.

Arriving in Toubkal National Park

Best time to visit The best time for walking is after the main snows, at blossom time in the spring. Mules cannot negotiate passes until March/April. For some, summers are too hot and visibility in the heat haze is poor. November to February is too cold, and there is too much snow for walking, although frozen ground is often more comfortable than walking on the ever-moving scree. Deep snows and ice present few problems to those with ropes, ice axes, crampons and experience. Without these, stay away in winter.

Information It's wise to purchase specialist hiking books (such as Alan Palmer's *Moroccan Atlas*) and maps. Mules and guides can be hired in Imlil, most easily in the Refuge. Having a local Tachelhit-speaking guide is essential on treks.

Imlil

Imlil, 17 km south-southeast from Asni, is the most important village of the Aït Mizane Valley. At 1790 m, it is the start of the walks in this area and is also a good place to hang out for a while. In the centre of the village is the car park/taxi area, with the stone-built **Club Alpin Français (CAF)** hut at the corner of the road, a guides hut and the **Café du Soleil**. There are small cafés and shops, a good baker, a highly recommended spice shop and a travel agent. Mules are 'parked' to the south of the village. There is a utilitarian concrete route indicator on the right, should you be unsure of your direction. When you arrive, you may be besieged by lots of underemployed blokes, keen to help you in some way or other. The town's **hammam** has been built with money from the kasbah (see page 94) and is recommended. Information in Imlil is available through the **Hôtel-Café Soleil** and at the **CAF refuge**.

Setti Fatma and the Ourika Valley → *For listings, see pages 93-97.*

The Ourika Valley is a beautiful area of steep-sided gorges and green, terraced fields along the winding Oued Ourika, about 45 minutes' drive south of Marrakech. The accessibility of the valley makes it a very popular excursion for Marrakchis and tourists, and, in summer, sections of the valley get crowded with campers and day trippers happy to be away from the hot, dusty air of the plain. Just before Aghbalou, the P2017 splits, with a right-hand road taking you up to the ski resort of Oukaïmeden. The trail-head village of Setti Fatma is reached by going straight ahead. The valley has occasional problems with flash floods, the worst of which, in 1995, destroyed most of Setti Fatma and killed many people.

Setti Fatma

The road ends at Setti Fatma, famous for its seven waterfalls and 100-year-old walnut trees. There is a small weekly market, a **Bureau des Guides de Montagne** and a good choice of basic accommodation and riverside tagine outlets. Setti Fatma must once have been idyllic. There is breeze-block housing among the older stone homes now, but the stunning setting and the sound of the river make it picturesque nonetheless. The place is set up primarily for Moroccan rather than European visitors, but that gives it an unusual charm, and Setti Fatma would be a good starting point for a trek (see below). It also makes a great day trip from Marrakech.

The main part of Setti Fatma stretches beyond the end of the road. Precarious temporary rope bridges wobble visitors and locals carrying sheep across to a large number of café-restaurants along the bank. The seven cascades are a 30-minute scramble up from Setti Fatma, following the path up behind the first café, and there are plenty of young men and children who will help you find the way. There is another café beside the first waterfall.

Setti Fatma makes a good base for exploring the **Jbel Yagour**, a plateau region famed for its numerous prehistoric rock carvings. See page 96 for trekking details.

Oukaïmeden

Oukaïmeden, 'the meeting place of the four winds', is Morocco's premier ski resort, and Africa's highest. It's some 2600 m up in the Atlas and a 1½-hour drive from Marrakech, making it a good day trip. The highest lift goes up to 3250 m, and there are various runs

---

down, not always very well marked. There are also four drag lifts and a tobogganing area. The resort is open for skiing from December to March but in summer it's less busy and many places are closed.

The quality of skiing is variable and good skiable snow cannot be counted on, though there's new investment and talk of snow cannons. The hot African sun means that the snow melts easily, only to freeze again at night, leaving slopes icy. Instructors work in the resort, and there are ski shops that rent equipment out and donkeys to carry your gear between lifts

Jbel Toubkal region

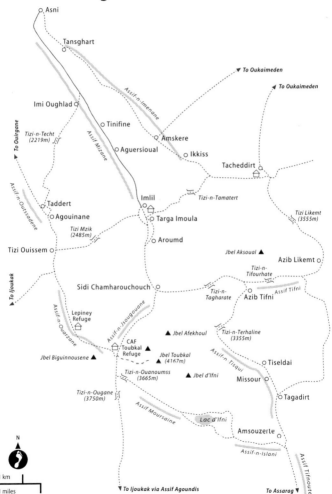

Walking in Toubkal

It's important to find a guide for longer walks as conditions can be dangerous. The number of people who have to drop out of treks in the area due to stomach problems is high, so try to check on hygiene when deciding who to use. If you're planning a trek in advance, **Mountain Voyage** (www.mountain-voyage.com), based in Marrakech, is recommended; see page 66.

Walking options include the **Aremd circuit**, a refreshing hike through remote villages with breathtaking views, and a hike to the **Lac d'Ifni**. Another is to walk to **Setti Fatma**, in the Ourika Valley.

Much more challenging is to climb **Jbel Toubkal**, the highest mountain in North Africa at 4167 m. It is necessary to break the walk at the **Club Alpin Français Toubkal Refuge** (ex-Refuge Neltner), a simple dormitory place with no meals at 3106 m. In winter this is a difficult trek and full equipment is essential. A specialist hiking book, such as Richard Knight's *Trekking in the Moroccan Atlas* (Hindhead: Trailblazer, 2008), is recommended. Mules and guides can be hired in Imlil, most easily in the Refuge (see Where to stay, page 94).

Imlil to Jbel Toubkal

Day1 Imlil is the end of the surfaced road but it is possible to reach **Aremd** (also spelt Aroumd) by car up the rough track. It takes about 45 minutes to walk. **Café Lac d'Ifni** makes a good stop here. **Sidi Chamharouchouch** is reached in another 2½ hours, going steadily uphill. It is important to bear right after the *marabout* to find the initially very steep, but later steady, slope up to the **Toubkal Refuge** (3207 m). Allow 4½ hours from Imlil. The Toubkal Refuge, with dormitory space for 30 people, 80dh per night, 150dh in summer, is often crowded. On the plus side, the warden sells bottled water, soft drinks, and can do food (50dh for a tagine). Campers using the level site below the hut can also use the facilities.

Day 2 The usual approach for walkers is via the South Cwm, a long day's walking and scrambling if you want to go up and back. The route is clearer on the map than it is on the ground. First observe the route from the rear of the **Toubkal Refuge**; the large boulders on the skyline are a point to aim for. Leave the refuge

In summer, visitors can walk, climb and even paraglide here. Look out for the prehistoric carvings on the rocky outcrop below the dam wall. There are further carvings on the flat rocks among the new chalets.

Towards Ouarzate via Tizi-n-Tichka

Completed in 1936 by the Foreign Legion, the N9 road from Marrakech to Ouarzazate gives stunning views. It runs through the full range of Atlas environments, from the Haouz plains, through the verdant foothills of the Oued Zat, to the barren peaks of the Atlas and the arid regions to the south. Drivers need maximum concentration on this route, especially in the twilight, when you will meet donkeys and flocks of sheep wandering across the road, guided by small children. Clapped out local buses break down, and there are some especially narrow and vertiginous stretches leading up to the pass after Taddert. A further hazard is the group of eager fossil sellers who hang out at viewpoints and café stops. Note that in winter there can be heavy cloud, snow storms and icy rain, reducing visibility and making the road extremely slippery. In such conditions, the road is not much fun at night. If snow cuts the pass, the snow barriers and go down to the river. Cross over and go up the other side to the main path to the foot of the first of the many screes. Take the scree path up to the boulders, which can be reached in just over an hour. From here, there is a choice: the long scree slope to the north of the summit, or the shorter, steeper slope to the south of the summit ridge. Either way, allow 3½ hours.

The summit is not in itself attractive but the stone shelters make fairly comfortable overnight camping for a good view of sunrise. Views are excellent – if there is no haze – to the Jbels Saghro and Siroua but, as the summit here (4167 m) is a plateau, other views are limited. Be prepared for low temperatures at this altitude and for the bitter winds that blow three out of four days in the spring and autumn. The descent is quicker; allow 2-2½ hours.

Toubkal Circuit

In nine days, a good walking circuit can give you a feel for life in the High Atlas and take in Jbel Toubkal too. The map (page 89) shows the main overnights.

Day 1 would take you from Imi Oughlad or Aguersioual to **Amskere**. On **Day 2**, the first full day getting used to the mountains, a five-hour trek takes you to **Tacheddirt**. A long **Day 3** runs via the Tizi Likemt (3555 m) to **Azib Likemt**. From here, you have another long **Day 4** over to **Amsouzerte**, where there is a difficult-to-find gîte or Landrover taxis back down to Marrakech. From Amsouzerte, on **Day 5**, you head for **Lac Ifni** (2290 m). **Day 6** takes you to the **Toubkal Refuge** (3106 m), via the Tizi-n-Ouanoumss (3665 m), and a long **Day 7** is the climb up **Jbel Toubkal** and back down to the refuge. **Day 8** takes you down to **Aroumd/Aremd** (1920 m), via the shrine of Sidi Chamharouch (2340 m) and its tiny collection of stalls. At the time of the pilgrimage, this shrine is very busy. From Aremd, on **Day 9**, you head back to Imi Oughlad (1300 m). This last long stretching of the legs takes you via the Tizi Oussem (1850 m) and the small settlements of Agouinane and Taddert before the last pass, Tizi-n-Techt (2219 m), taking you down to **Imi Oughlad**.

will be down. The total distance from Marrakech to Ouarzazate is nearly 200 km. Good places to stop include upper **Taddert** (busy, 86 km from Marrakech), the **Tizi-n-Tichka** pass (2260 m) itself, which is almost exactly halfway, or **Ighrem-n-Ouagdal**, about 118 km from Marrakech, where there is an old *agadir* (granary) to visit. Driving in good conditions, Marrakech to Taddert will take you two hours, while Taddert to Ouarzazate is about another two.

Telouet

An eagle's nest of a place, high in the mountains, Telouet is something of a legend. It has one of the most spectacular kasbahs in the Atlas. Today, it is on the tourist circuit, as the hordes of 4WD vehicles testify. Within living memory, however, its name was synonymous with the repressive rule of the Glaoui brothers.

The history of Telouet and its kasbah is short but bloodthirsty. It is the story of how two brothers of the Glaoua tribe, sons of an Ethiopian slave woman, by force of arms and character, managed to achieve absolute dominance over much of southern Morocco in the early 20th century. Gavin Maxwell's *Lords of the Atlas* describes the turbulent times in Marrakech and the mountains, as first the Moroccan monarchy and then the French skirmished with the southern tribal leaders to achieve dominance. The denouement, which came shortly after Moroccan Independence in 1956, was fatal to Glaoui power.

Abandoned before completion, the Kasbah of Telouet as it survives today is mainly the result of 20th-century building schemes by the last great Glaoui lord, T'hami. Generally, as you arrive, someone will emerge to show you around. The great reception rooms, with their cedar ceilings and crumbling stucco, a transposition of 19th-century Moroccan urban taste to the mountains, are worth a visit.

Telouet to Ouarzazate via Aït Ben Haddou

For those with 4WD, Telouet is also the starting point for an 80-km route down to Ouarzazate. Ask for the road to Animiter, the first main village. Leaving Telouet, after a few kilometres, a turn-off to the left, near the foot of Jbel Amassine, takes you up to the source of the Glaoui family's wealth, a salt mine. **Animiter**, some 9 km east from Telouet, was famous in the early days of Moroccan tourism as its kasbah, painted by Jacques Majorelle, was featured on an early poster. Here the surfaced road runs out. It should be possible to camp near the Oued Mellah. The next village, **Timsal**, lies a few kilometres to the south. After Timsal, follow the track along the Adrar Taqqat, used when they put in electricity lines. You reach **Tioughassine**, and the track follows the Ounila Valley. At **Assaka**, look out for abandoned granaries under the cliffs. The track then follows up onto a sort of plateau above the canyon. Next, the main track drops steeply down to the valley bottom; **Tizgui-n-Barda** is the next main village, about 29 km from Telouet. Continue along the Assif Ounila to reach **Tamdacht**, meeting point of the *oueds* Marghene and Ounila and the start of the surfaced road. The next stop, **Aït Ben Haddou**, is 50 km from Telouet.

This route was used in earlier times by caravans coming up from the south to pick up salt from the Telouet mine. Today, it is increasingly popular as an off-road excursion. In wet weather parts of the track turn to red-clay mud, difficult if you get stuck. As with other off-road adventures, it should be tackled by vehicles in pairs. If you get stuck, you will definitely need someone to help dig you out of trouble.

Western High Atlas listings

For hotel and restaurant price codes and other
relevant information, see pages 10-16.

🛏 Where to stay

Lalla Takerkoust *p84*
€€ **Le Flouka**, Barrage Lalla Takerkoust,
T0664-492660, www.leflouka.com.
14 rooms are scattered around **Le Flouka**,
right at the water's edge of Lalla Takerkoust.
Comfortable rooms are simply decorated
with lamps and rugs and there are bare
beams and open fires. There are also
simpler tents and a de luxe *tente de pacha*,
with a built-in bathroom. Of the 2 pools,
one is reserved for hotel guests, though
you can just as easily head straight out
into the lake. Swimming straight towards
the Atlas mountains is hard to beat. There
is a restaurant (€€) right beside the lake,
serving dishes such as steak or mozzarella
and tomato salad, as well as a bar, but it's
a peaceful spot, big enough to absorb its
visitors with laid-back ease.

Amizmiz *p85*
Before you reach Amizmiz, there are several
options for an overnight stop, including **Le
CaravanSerai** (€), at Ouled Ben Rahmoun,
see page 54.

Asni *p85*
€€€€ **Kasbah Tamadot**, T0208-600 0430
(UK), T877-577 8777 (USA) or T0524-368200
(Morocco), www.kasbahtamadot.com.
One of Morocco's best-known hotels,
Kasbah Tamadot is run by Virgin and
calls itself 'Sir Richard Branson's Moroccan
Retreat', though chances are you won't
bump into him here. Complete with all
the creature comforts you can imagine,
the cheapest of the 18 rooms is more than
3000dh a night and for your investment you
get indoor and outdoor pools, gardens, spa
and a hammam, as well as some spectacular
views. The restaurant uses ingredients from

the hotel's own gardens and the library
comes equipped with a telescope. Despite
all its good points, however, it has a little less
character than its two rivals, **Kasbah Toubkal**
and **Kasbah Bab Ourika**.

Ouirgane *p86*
€€€ **Chez Momo II**, coming from
Marrakech, 800 m past **La Roseraie**,
up a road on the left, T0524-485704,
aubergemomo.com. After the original
Chez Momo was engulfed in the water
of Ouirgane's new reservoir in 2008, **Chez
Momo II** was born, further up the hill, using
local craftsmen and materials. Rooms are
homely and elegant, with wrought-iron
beds, bare wooden beams and lamps
in alcoves. There's a beautiful horseshoe
arch pool at the front of the house, with
trees, roses and sun loungers around, and
'trikking', on foot or on mule, is organized.
€€ **Auberge Au Sanglier Qui Fume**,
T0524-485707, www.ausanglierquifume.
com. A small country hotel run by a French
couple, 'the boar that smokes' has 22
chalet-style rooms, a restaurant serving
excellent French country food, a bar, tennis
court and a pool in the summer. There are
mountain bikes and quad bikes for rent,
and the management will put you in touch
with guides should you wish to do some
walking or horse riding. The titular boar,
complete with pipe, watches over the bar.
€€ **La Bergerie**, about 2 km before
Ouirgane village as you come from
Marrakech, turn right at the signpost for
Marigha, T0524-485717, www.labergerie-
maroc.com. Particularly well set up for
families, French-run La Bergerie is spread
amongst 5 ha of grounds in a valley away
from the village. The restaurant serves a
good mix of French and Moroccan food,
combining dishes such as kefta and egg
tagine with apricots and goat's cheese.
There's beer on tap and a good outdoor
seating area, and they'll even knock up a

fondue on request. The best rooms are the bungalows set in the grounds, with some privacy and more style, nicely worn old furniture and private gardens with peach, apricot and apple trees.

€€ La Roseraie, T0524-439128, www.la roseraiehotel.com. A peaceful hotel set in a 25 ha of exceptionally colourful rose gardens, with 42 rooms and suites, 2 restaurants, a bar next to the pool and 2 tennis courts. The rooms, however, are less spectacular than the gardens, with rather dated peach bathrooms. Horse riding is organized.

Imlil and the Toubkal National Park
p87, map p89

The **Bureau des Guides**, in the centre of Imlil, can provide information on accommodation in homes: locals, who are used to walkers, are generally keen to provide a floor or mattresses to sleep on.

€€€€ Kasbah du Toubkal, T0524-485611, Imlil, www.kasbahdutoubkal. com. Imlil's restored kasbah, perched spectacularly above the village, played the role of a Tibetan fortress in director Martin Scorsese's film *Kundun*. It is run by the UK-based travel agent **Discover Ltd** in conjunction with locals and is often cited as a good example of eco-tourism. There is a range of accommodation, from 3 dorms for groups to 5 deluxe rooms. The best rooms come with CD players, slippers and even Berber clothes to borrow. The building, once HQ of the local *caïd*, is worth a visit; for a 20dh contribution to the local development fund, you can have mint tea and walnuts on the roof terrace. A day trip to the Kasbah can also be arranged form Marrakech for €85, including lunch, a mule ride and a visit to a Berber house.

€€ Riad Imlil, Imlil, T0524-485485, T0661-240599 (mob), www.riaddecharme-imlil. com. Good rooms with TV, room service, Wi-Fi, fridges and a/c. Stone and *tadelakt* are both used, though the rooms are a little dark. There's a restaurant with a fire and a small 'salon Berbere'.

€ Auberge El Aine, Imlil, T0524-485662, T0666-647999 (mobile), iframed@hotmail. com. On the right as you arrive in the village from Asni, this is a bargain. Rooms are small but cute, with windows opening onto a garden with cherry blossom in spring. It's friendly, and the bright colours, topsy turvy stairs and a big tree in the courtyard give the place extra character. Upstairs rooms are best, or there are small apartments with bathroom and kitchen, good for families or small groups.

€ Auberge Imi N'Ouassif, Chez Mohammed Bouinbaden, Imlil, T0524-485126, T0662-105126 (mob), iminouassif@ wanadoo.ma. On the western outskirts of the town, along paths between high stone walls, this is a simple, quiet place that also provides guides.

€ Gite Atlas Aremd, Aremd, T0668-882764, atlastreking@yahoo.ca. Mustapha Ibdlaid runs this basic gîte in Aremd with 12 rooms and good views across the valley to the mountains. There's the option to sleep on sofas in the salon. Hot showers included.

€ Gite Id Mansour, Aremd, T0524-485613, T0662-355214 (mob). A good gite in Aremd, **Id Mansour** has hot water and towels and is very clean. Beds are comfortable and new and some rooms have mountain views. Stark but fairly comfortable.

€ Refuge du Club Alpin Français, Imlil, T0524-485122, T0677-307415 (mob). Minimal facilities but clean and with a very friendly welcome and good information from Lydia, the French manager. 40 beds in dorms, open all year round.

Setti Fatma and Ourika Valley *p88*

€€€€ Kasbah Bab Ourika, 45 mins from Marrakech off the Setti Fatma road near Dar-Caid-Ouriki, T0524-389797, T0661-252328 (mob), www.babourika. com. Unfussily elegant, this kasbah is in an extraordinary location, perched on its own personal hill overlooking the mouth of the Ourika valley, with craggy red mountain rock to one side and Marrakech in the distance behind. Built, set up and run by the owner of **Riad Edward** in Marrakech, this place is decorated with a similar insouciant style: rooms are huge and have an antique, rustic atmosphere that makes guests feel immediately at home but are also luxurious, with thick rugs, generous bathrooms, open fires and wonderfully comfortable beds. The pool is spectacular, with views to the mountains, and the food is exquisite, with dishes such as chilled carrot soup and lemongrass beef brochette with stir-fried spinach and turmeric expertly mixing flavours. The environmental and social policies of the place are ground-breaking, and guests can take a guided walk through the extraordinarily fertile valley and Berber villages below. The track that needs to be navigated to reach the front door is an eroded adventure, but one that increases the dramatic sense of arrival, and of being in a very special place indeed.

€€ Dar Piano, T0524-484842, T0661-342884 (mob), www.darpiano.com. Closed Jun-Aug. On the right of the road from Marrakech, about 10 km south of Setti Fatma, this cosy, French-run place has simple, homely rooms, good cooking and roof terrace views.

€€ La Perle d'Ourika, T0661 56 72 39, laperledourika@hotmail.com. A couple of minutes downstream from Setti Fatma, the **Perle** has a degree of decoration rare in Setti Fatma, with furry sequined bed covers and painted floors. It's a little over the top, but it is at least an attempt at style. Good shared facilities, 24-hr hot water and a roof terrace with fantastic views up and down the valley. The restaurant is also recommended and has wine.

€ Azilal, Setti Fatma, T0668-883770. Next to **Hotel Asgaour**, this is a bright and cheerful place, lacking in some creature comforts and with small rooms but with hot water and views over the river. For those on a tight budget, there's a big room you can sleep in for 30dh each.

€ Evasion, Setti Fatma, T0666-640758. Near the bottom of the village, on the opposite side from the river, this is a modern place with good rooms, as long as you're not too disturbed by the strange blue blurry glass. There are balconies with views over the valley and good bathrooms. The attached café has a proper coffee machine and a glassed-in room for rainy days.

€ Hotel Asgaour, Setti Fatma, T0524-485294, T0666-416419 (mob). A friendly place with 20 basic, clean rooms and small but comfy beds. Some rooms have views over the valley, and the hotel has a pretty terrace across the other side of the river, as well as some chairs and tables outside. Rooms with private shower and toilet are more expensive.

Oukaïmeden *p88*

Oukaïmeden has a small but adequate supply of accommodation. In practice, the resort only gets crowded on snowy weekends, and many visitors from Marrakech prefer to return home to sleep. Out of season, rooms in mountain chalets can be found.

€€ Chez Juju, T0524 319005, www.hotelchezjuju.com. Open all year (except Ramadan). 8 clean and well looked-after wood-clad rooms, with a decent restaurant serving French as well as Moroccan cuisine, and a bar with cold beer. Half-board is obligatory.

€€ Hotel Kenzi Louka, T0524-319080. Open all year round. A large, triangular-shaped hotel, with fairly basic but comfortable rooms. Outside pool (generally heated), information and advice on skiing and trekking.

€ Refuge of the Club Alpin Francais, T0524-319036. Open all year. Dorm bunks as well as private double rooms. Skiing equipment, mountain bikes, etc, can be hired and there's a bar and games room.

Telouet *p91*

€ Auberge Ouahsous, Anguelz, T0661-199400, www.auberge-ouahsous.com.

10 km from Telouet in the direction of Aït Ben Haddou, this rather imposing hotel has simple, clean, comfortable, rooms, some en suite, a restaurant and a grocery store open 0700-2300.

🍴 Restaurants

Hardly anywhere in the Atlas operates just as a restaurant, though there are cafés, and most hotels also serve food.

Asni *p85*
In the centre of the village are a number of stalls and cafés cooking harira soup and tagines. This is the last major place to stock up on basic supplies for a visit to the Toubkal region.

Ouirgane *p86*
The hotels in Ouirgane all have restaurants attached; **La Bergerie** is a good stopover for lunch.

Tizi-n-Test *p87*
For a nearby lunch stop, the cheap **Restaurant La Belle Vue** (boumzough. free.fr) is about 1 km after the pass on the Taroudant side.

Imlil and the Toubkal National Park
p88, map p89
Most places offer half board, so the standalone eating options are limited, but **Café Soleil** and **Atlas Tichka** offer good lunches. **Les Amis** does good chicken brochettes and genuine coffee; **Café Grand Atlas** is more of a local place, where you can eat tagine on the roof terrace. **Café Imlil** was the first café in town and hasn't changed much since. For something smarter, and for the best views, go to the **Kasbah de Toubkal**.

Setti Fatma and Ourika Valley *p88*
There are a huge number of places in Setti Fatma that set up to catch the lunchtime trade from Marrakech, offering excellent tagines freshly cooked at stalls near the river. There's little to choose between them; wander around and pick one that smells good, or go for a table with a view.

Oukaïmeden *p88*
Chez Juju is probably the best option.

⏱ What to do

Imlil and the Toubkal National Park
p88, map p89
Tours and guides
Reckon on about 350dh per day per person and tip generously; about 50dh a day is probably about right.
Brahim Ait Zin, T0667-690903, trekadventurer@yahoo.fr. Brahim knows the mountains very well and speaks good English.
Bureau des Guides, in the centre of Imlil, T0524-485626, bureau.guides@yahoo. fr. Daily 0700-1900 summer, 0800-1700 winter. You can find a guide here.
Hassan Agafay, T0667-842236 (mob). Also recommended is this local outfit.

Setti Fatma and Ourika Valley *p88*
Rafting
Splash Rafting Morocco, Albakech House, Av Mohammed VI, Agdal, Marrakech, T0618-964252, moroccoadventuretours. com. The best rafting conditions are in the winter and spring. Class III and IV whitewater rafting takes place in the Ourika Valley Dec-May. Splash also run 3-day rafting trips to the Ahansal river Mar-Jun. 650dh per person for a half-day rafting trip.

Trekking
About 10 km from Setti Fatma is Tachedirt, where there is a Refuge du CAF. To set up a trek, contact the **Bureau des Guides de Montagne**, on your right before the hotels. The place is run by the very capable, and English-speaking Abderrahim ('Abdou') Mandili, T0524-291308, T0668-562340 (mob), abdoumandili@yahoo.fr.

⊖ Transport

Trips out from Marrakech into the Western High Atlas are fairly easy using buses or shared taxis. In order to do much moving about between villages, your own transport is invaluable, however. Once in the mountains, many of the roads are narrow and winding, with vertiginous drops.

Asni *p85*
There are regular buses, and much quicker *grands taxis*, to Bab Rob in **Marrakech** (2½ hrs).

Tin Mal and Tizi-n-Test *p86 and p87*
The R203 road leaves Marrakech heading south through various small villages on its way to Tin Mal and the Tizi-n-Test pass before dropping down again to Taroudant, gateway to the south, beyond. Tin Mal is about 2 hrs' drive from **Marrakech**, taking things easy, 8 km past the village of Ijoukak. You can also take a Taroudant bus or a grand taxi as far as Ijoujak, where there are several basic cafés with rooms. The pass is another 37 km further southwest.

Setti Fatma and Ourika Valley *p88*
Buses and *grands taxis* go to Bab Rob in **Marrakech**. If driving from Marrakech, head straight for the mountains on the P2017, starting from the fountain roundabout just outside the city walls at Bab Jedid, next to the Hotel Mamounia. Once in Ourika, a possible means of transport is a lift in the open-top vans and lorries which speed along the valley.

Oukaïmeden *p88*
Daily buses to **Marrakech** in winter. From Marrakech, it's reached via the P2017 Ourika Valley road, but forking right 43 km out of Marrakech, instead of left for Setti Fatma. Another option is to walk the piste which leaves the road south of Oukaïmeden, and cross the hills to the R203 to south of Asni.

In a 4WD, you can take winding roads and tracks to **Tahanaoute** and **Asni** on the R203 Tizi-n-Test road. Although the villages and landscapes are beautiful, the villages are very poor, and children are eager for pens, notebooks and dirhams (see box, page 85). When you pull away from a village, watch out that none are clinging onto the back of your vehicle for a thrilling (if dangerous) dare.

Telouet *p91*
A narrow road, in need of resurfacing and with nasty tyre-splitting edges, takes you from the Tizi-n-Tichka road to Telouet; turn left 106 km from Marrakech. For those without their own vehicle, the trip is problematic, though there may be grands taxis up from Ighrem-n-Ouagdal, or you could hire a driver in Marrakech.

Eastern High Atlas

A mountainous hinterland with little of the infrastructure of the Atlas around Toubkal, the Atlas to the east of Marrakech is a wild and little-visited area, with towns along its northern edge, strung out along the N8 from Marrakech to Fès.

Well watered like the High Atlas of Toubkal, the High Atlas south of Azilal has a very different character, due perhaps to the inaccessibility of its valleys, hidden away in the heart of the mountains. The people here are Tamazight-speaking, and more limited contact with mainstream Morocco makes them more conservative. Formal education has had little impact in the high valleys and it was only in the late 1990s that roads began to replace some of the rough tracks. Much of the region's attraction comes from the architecture of the villages, largely unspoiled by concrete. There is also more vegetation here than further west, with conifer forests surviving at high altitude. As well as wide flat valleys, there are deep gorges and small rivers that can easily turn to flood after a rainstorm on the mountains. The highest mountain in the region is the long, rounded ridge of the Ighil Mgoun, which reaches 4071 m.

The town of Azilal gives access to both the beautiful, remote high valley of the Aït Bougmez, an area increasingly popular with walkers, and the Cascades d'Ouzoud, Morocco's highest waterfall. Other attractions include the natural stone bridge of Imi-n-Ifri near Demnate.

Further east is an area of shoulder mountains, snowcapped into early summer, bare plateaux, occasional deep canyons and semi-nomad lifestyles in the high pastures. Gone are the long, deep, winding valleys of the Western mountains, with their terraced fields; highlights include the Jbel Ayyachi and the deep gorges of the Assif Melloul, thick with vegetation.

Imilchil is the most obvious 'capital' of this area and trekking expeditions set off from here. The region is particularly beautiful in late spring, when the greens of young barley and poplars coming into leaf contrast with the creamy-brown nakedness of the cliff-sides above. Near to Imilchil are the calm twin lakes of Isli and Tislit. Tracks lead across the mountains to another major meeting of the ways, Zaouïat Ahansal.

Azilal and the Aït Bougmez Valley

Demnate and Imi-n-Ifri → For listings, see pages 103-105.
On the R210 about 1½ hours from Marrakech. Demnate was once a picturesque, whitewashed place. These days the crumbling kasbah, once set in the middle of olive groves, is surrounded by unsightly new building. Nearby, **Imi-n-Ifri** ('the door to the cave') is a natural rock bridge formed by the partial collapse of a huge cavern. If you don't have transport, there are transit vans that do the short run up from Demnate. Opposite the closed auberge of the same name, a path winds down to the stream bed and a small reservoir where it's possible to swim and camp. Concrete steps, partly gone, take you up to the **grotto**. Above your head, there are great sheets of calcareous rock and, above that, cawing choughs circling overhead. You may also see the odd Barbary squirrel.

Cascades d'Ouzoud
These waterfalls, about 2½ hours' drive away from Marrakech, make a long day trip. The left turn off the R304, about 20 km before Azilal, is signposted. Tumbling 110 m down cliffs and red with clay after heavy rains, the Cascades d'Ouzoud are an impressive sight and can be seen from above as well as below. The word *ouzoud* comes from the Amazigh *izide*, meaning delicious. After the turn-off from the R304, the road heads north through beautiful landscapes where the dominant colours are red earth, dark green thuya and the paler grey green of the olive trees. Arriving in the village of Ouzoud, various local men will emerge waving sticks to help you park. For the cascades, head past the riad, and a few metres of market garden land crossed by rivulets of fast-flowing water lead you to the edge of the precipice (watch out for slippery clay). Look out for the traditional water-driven barley mills. There are various paths that will take you down to cafés on the rocks below the falls. It's possible to swim at the base of the falls, but be careful diving in, as the pool is shallow.

Azilal
Sprawling west from a small core of kasbah and French military buildings, terracotta red Azilal is less of a one-mule place than it used to be. In fact, it is turning into a major town with stilt-legged buildings, a big *gare routière*, several hotels (see page 103), a Thursday souk and a **tourist office** ⓘ *Av Hassan II, T0523-488334*. From Azilal it is a slow 2¾-hour drive south over the mountains into the Aït Bougmez.

Vallée des Aït Bougmez → For listings, see pages 103-105.
The Aït Bougmez is one of the most beautiful valleys of the High Atlas, so far unspoiled by breeze-block building. Electricity arrived in early 2001, and the completion of the black-top road will bring further changes. The stone- and *pisé*-built villages above the fields of the valley bottom are fine examples of housing, perfectly adapted to local environment and needs. One of the most isolated regions of the High Atlas, the Aït Bougmez was

Moussem des fiançailles

Imilchil is famous for its annual summer wedding festival, Moussem des fiançailles, which was traditionally an occasion for people from all over the region to get together. The moussem site is in fact at Allamghou, signed left off the route from Rish, some 20 km before Imilchil and near the meeting place with the mountain piste up from Tinghir.

The local legend goes that two young people fell in love and wanted to marry. Their parents said no, and the couple cried so much that two lakes formed: Tislit for the girl, and Isli for the bridegroom. With such results, the parents could hardly continue to refuse and allowed their offspring to choose the partner of their choice. The moussem became a great occasion for locals to turn out in all their finery and celebrate marriages with plenty of traditional dances and singing.

In recent years, the occasion has suffered from the incursions of tourists – and drought. In all of Morocco's rural communities, weddings – expensive, once-in-a-lifetime occasions that they are – require a lot of available capital, which always in short supply in drought years. Nevertheless, in villages along the route to Imilchil, there is some new prosperity, lots of new building, for the most part using traditional packed-earth construction methods.

until recently annually cut off by snow for part of the winter. Though walking groups are beginning to make a contribution to the local economy, life is still hard.

Tabant, 1850 m up, is the main centre, and the wide, flat-bottomed valley provides pleasant some excellent walking out from here. You could find a local to walk you up to the dinosaur footsteps near Rbat. Tabant to Agouti is an easy 8-km walk along the valley road; look out for the granary of Sidi Moussa up on a mound-like hill. There is another, slightly longer route from Tabant to Ifrane along the old main piste to Aït M'hamed. Longer, more serious treks, head to the **Massif du Mgoun**, Morocco's second-highest mountain massif.

Massif du Mgoun

Although not the most aesthetically pleasing of mountains (it has no soaring peaks), Mgoun has the largest area of land above 3000 m in the whole country. The best time to climb the mountain is probably summer or early autumn, for snow remains late into the year in these highlands. The easiest route to the summit is from the south side of the mountain, which means starting from El Kelaâ des Mgouna in the Dadès Valley. The alternative is to head south from the Aït Bougmez to approach the massif from the east. Taking this option, head south from **Tabant** over the Tizi-n-Aït Imi (2905 m) to **Tighremt-n-Aït Ahmed**, and then west to the foot of the mountain along the course of the Assif Oulliliymt on a second day's trek. The ascent to the highest point (4071 m) is not actually difficult. Note that the summit is sacred: in a survival of pre-Islamic tradition, the mountain's help (protection) may be asked, even today.

A popular hiking option is to trek from the Aït Bougmez south to **Bou Thrarar** and **Kelaât Mgouna**. This is a six-day trip, with possible camps at Tarzout, Aguerzka and Bou Thrarar. It will be up to your guide to break up the route as they see fit. Apart from the high pass on the first day, there are no huge climbs, and you will be walking for between six and seven hours a day.

Beni Mellal and around → *For listings, see pages 103-105.*

One of the major centres of central Morocco, Beni Mellal, on the northern edge of the Atlas, has an important souk on Tuesday. Like a number of other towns in the region, it has grown thanks largely to money sent back by migrant workers in Italy. The main monuments include the **Kasbah Bel Kush**. Built in the 17th century by Moulay Ismaïl, it was heavily restored in the 19th century. It's also worth a walk up to the small, quiet **gardens** below the ruined Kasbah de Ras el Aïn, perched precariously on the cliffside. There is a nice café in the gardens. The **tourist office** ① *1st floor of Immeuble Chichaoui, Av Hassan II, T0523 48 39 81.*

Kasbah Tadla

Kasbah Tadla, to the northeast of Beni Mellal, was founded in 1687 by the Alaouite Sultan Moulay Ismaïl, no doubt because it is ideally located more or less halfway between Marrakech and Meknès and Fès, the imperial cities of the Saïss Plain. The crumbling terracotta ramparts sit above the shrivelled course of the river and, except for a new social-housing project on the flood plain, the view is little changed since the town's foundation. On the 'plateau' behind the kasbah is a rather derelict public garden, splendid in a quiet sort of way when the purple jacarandas are in flower. Within the kasbah there is a lot of self-built housing, put up by soldiers and their families, and two mosques, one with the distinctive Almohad lozenge design on the minaret. The other has poles protruding from the minaret. Someone might offer to show you into the courtyard building behind the mosque, which was the sultan's residence. Today, it is inhabited by poor residents. The 10-arched bridge over the Oum er Rbia is a fine example of 17th-century engineering. Kasbah Tadla's souk day is Monday.

The best view of the kasbah is from the austere **monument** to four resistance heroes on a low rise on the south side of the town. Four parallel concrete blades rise skywards, but there is no inscription to recall who the heroes were.

Boujaâd

Just a 25-minute drive from Kasbah Tadla, Boujaâd is something of a surprise. In recent memory, it was an important town – essentially a pilgrimage centre for the semi-nomadic inhabitants of the Tadla plain. The historic medina has an almost Mediterranean character, with its arcaded square, whitewashed walls, shrines, paved streets and white houses. Much of the town was destroyed in 1785. The key buildings are the **Zaouïa of Sidi Othman** and the **Mosque of Sidi Mohammed Bu'abid ech Cherki**, the town's founder.

Trekking from Imilchil to Anergui and Zaouïat Ahansal

→ *For listings, see pages 103-105.*

One of the best treks in the Atlas takes you from the plateaux of the Imilchil region, via the Assif Melloul and the beautiful village of Anergui, to the former pilgrimage centre of Zaouïat Ahansal. This route, part of the **Grande traversée de l'Atlas marocain**, takes you through remote regions where knowledge of French (and even Arabic) will be rudimentary to say the least. Take a local, preferably Tabant-trained, guide, who will be aware of potentially snowy conditions (if travelling outside summer) and water levels in the Assif Melloul. At Zaouïat Ahansal, you link in with further routes southwest to the Aït Bougmez and north to the Cathedral Rocks of Tilouguite and Ouaouizaght. A number of European-based travel companies now do treks in this region. Accommodation is in mountain gîtes, camping out or in locals' homes.

Imilchil

Southeast of Kasbah Tadla, though marginally more easily approached from Rich to the east, Imilchil centres on a beautiful crumbling kasbah topped with storks' nests. The town has a dusty, sloping main street, where you will find a couple of small cafés, the local dispensary and the entrance to the souk. Behind the kasbah, the **Hotel Izlane** can provide a little information on possible treks and may be able to put you in contact with suitable guides. Quiet for most of the year, the town comes alive for the annual marriage fair in September (see box, page 100), when young people descend from the mountains to find themselves a partner.

Lac Tislit, 5 km to the north, is an exquisite if austere oval of blue ringed by reeds, set in an arid hollow of the mountains. The natural splendour is a little marred by a bogus kasbah, complete with plastic ceremonial tents. After Lac Tislit, the larger **Lac Isli** is an easy day's 4WD trip.

Imilchil to Anergui

There are various trek routes from Imilchil to Anergui, a distance of roughly 57 km. The route you take will depend on weather conditions. Some routes require better than average physical condition. If the **Assif Melloul** is not in flood, your guide will take you along the riverside route, which involves some wading and goes via the small settlements of Ouedddi and Oulghazi. After Oulghazi, you may head up out of the river valley to Anergui via the **Tizi-n-Echfart** pass. The other option is a more perilous route high above the river. The river will be in full flood in spring, and ice in shady areas can make high paths perilous for both people and mules.

With the green of its fruit and walnut trees, **Anergui** is one of the most beautiful sites in the eastern High Atlas and a place which now has some accommodation, see page 104.

Anergui to Zaouïat Ahansal

The Assif Melloul continues west from Anergui to meet the **Assif ou Ahansal** near the so-called **Cathedral Rocks** near Tamga. A basic track from Anergui to Zaouïat Ahansal can just about be crossed with 4WD, a distance of around 92 km. For walkers, this route is especially fine, taking you through the beautiful gorges of the Assif Melloul.

Zaouïat Ahansal

Zaouïat Ahansal (altitude 1600 m) became important due to its location at a meeting of the ways between the eastern and central High Atlas. There are a couple of gîtes. The easiest way to Zaouïat Ahansal is from Azilal, a distance of 83 km. There are fairly frequent 4WD taxis doing this run. About 17 km out of Azilal, a junction is reached where you either go right for the Aït Bougmez or left for Aït M'hamed (Saturday souk), 3 km further on. From here, it's another 63 km to Zaouïat Ahansal. The tarmac runs out a few kilometres out of Aït M'hamed, but the track continues east-southeast towards the **Tizi-n-Tsalli-n-Imenain** (2763 m, 50 km from Azilal), in the shelter of the great Jbel Azourki (3677 m). A further col, the **Tizi-n-Ilissi** (2600 m), comes 16 km further on, below Jbel Arroudane (3359 m). Then comes the drop down to Zaouïat Ahansal.

Eastern High Atlas listings

For hotel and restaurant price codes and other relevant information, see pages 10-16.

Where to stay

Demnate and Imi-n-Ifri *p99*
€€€ **Kasbah Timdaf**, T0523-507178, www.kasbah-timdaf.com. A beautiful ecolodge with traditionally designed Berber rooms, flower-filled gardens and a hammam. There's an open fire for when it's cold, free Wi-Fi and good food cooked by the French owners. Cookery lessons are available on request.
€€ **Tiziout Maison d'Hôtes**, just north of Demnate, T0658-346148, www.tizouit.ma. In a new building made from stone, an elegant but low-key place with 8 spacious, attractive rooms, a pool and great views.
€ **Gîte d'étape**, at Imi-n-Ifri, T0524-456473. Open only in summer. Take the right-hand fork past the café; it's signposted.
€ **Hotel Café d'Ouzoud**, on main Av Mohammed V, T0662-239972 (mob) or T0661-241099 (mob). 24 small clean rooms.

Cascades d'Ouzoud *p99*
€€ **Hotel Chellal d'Ouzoud**, T0523-429180, hotelchellal.weebly.com. A cheerful, colourful place with en suite rooms that are liberally decorated with rugs, fabrics and cushions.
€€ **Riad Cascades d'Ouzoud**, T0523-459658, www.ouzoud.com. The best accommodation option near the waterfalls, this riad has a combination of whitewashed and rough *pisé*-style walls, 9 tastefully decorated rooms and a spacious roof terrace with panoramic views over the surrounding countryside. There are wooden beamed ceilings and some rooms have open fireplaces. The riad also does decent food, both Moroccan and French, using good local ingredients, either on the terrace or in a traditional Moroccan lounge downstairs.
€ **Hotel de France**, T0523-459017. Cheap rooms, some of which have en suite bathrooms. Restaurant.

Camping
This is possible at various small sites but you might be better off on the roof terrace of one of the cheap hotels.

Azilal *p99*
€€ **Hotel Assounfou**, T0523-459220. Satellite TV and solar-heated water, which only partly explains why it is generally cold. Friendly and very pink.
€ **Hotel Dadès**, T0523-458245. Basic, 3-bed concrete box rooms, hot showers extra. Just as you arrive from Marrakech, on your right.

Vallée des Aït Bougmez *p99*
Options are limited in Tabant itself though a few attractive options have sprung up in other villages in the valley. In many villages there is simple sleeping space in gîtes.
€€€ **Dar Itrane**, Imelghas, T0523-459312, www.origins-lodge.com. One of the best options in the area is this fine, French-managed ecolodge, a traditional red adobe building 1800 m up near the village of Imeghas. There are 17 en suite rooms, a roof terrace, a hammam and a chef prepares local Berber dishes. The name means 'House of the Stars', and it so called because the remoteness of the place make it perfect for viewing the night sky.
€€ **La Casbah M-Goun**, Douar Agerd-n-ozro, T0662-778148, www.hotel-ait-bouguemez.com. There's a spectacular setting for this traditional place. Simple rooms are generously kitted out with rugs and blankets, and there are great views of the surrounding green fields and bare mountains.
€€ **Touda**, Zawyat Oulmzi. You wouldn't necessarily know it from the simple, traditional exterior, but this is a cut above most of most of the gîtes in Aït Bougmez, with *tadelakt* bathrooms and carefully designed bedrooms.

€ Gîte d'étape Imelghas, Imelghas, T0523-459341. The best of the cheap gîtes. Accommodation for up to 40, clean loos and showers.

Beni Mellal *p101*

€€ Hotel Ouzoud, Rte de Marrakech, T0523-483752, www.sogatour.ma. 28 rooms and suites with balconies in a modern but not especially attractive hotel with restaurant, bar, tennis and pool.

€ Hotel de l'Aïn-Asserdoun, Av des FAR, T0523-483493. A modern place with en suite bathrooms, balconies and a restaurant.

€ Hotel Marhaba, on the small square in the old town (reached by heading up the souk street which leads uphill to the right of the big ceremonial gates and square), T0523-483991. A simple option with 11 rooms around a courtyard. Option to sleep on roof terrace.

€ Hotel Tasmmet, in the older part of town, not that easy to find, but if you get onto the street which runs parallel to the main street behind the **CTM** offices you eventually see it down a side street to your left as you head towards the kasbah, T0523-421313. Rooms have en suite bathrooms and the best have balconies. You can also sleep cheaply on the roof terrace.

Boujaâd *p101*

€ Café-Hotel Essalyn, Pl du Marché, on the main square.

People on pilgrimages rent rooms in private houses near the shrines.

Imilchil *p102*

Options are few but adequate. Apart from the place listed below, there is some simple dorm accommodation in the village.

€ Hotel Izlane, clearly visible behind the kasbah, T0523-442806, www.hotelizlane. com. Run by mountain guide Khalla Boudrik, the hotel has a large restaurant, 15 rooms, 39 beds, 3 hot showers and 4 loos. Has regional maps and can advise on treks.

Anergui *p102*

€ Wihalane ('the right place'), pagesperso-orange.fr/wihalane. For information, contact Lahcen Fouzal on T0667-265319 via **Studio La Nature** in Ouaouizaght or via José Garcia, 17 Rue de Sermaize, 90000 Belfort, France, T+33-384266049.

🍴 Restaurants

Beni Mellal *p101*

Hotel de Paris, a little way out of the town centre on Kasbah Tadla road, T0523-282245. The restaurant serves alcohol.

Salon de Thé Azouhour, 241 Av Mohammed V.

There are also *laiteries* and cafés along the main street.

🚌 Transport

Azilal *p99*

Azilal is the transport hub for the regions of the High Atlas to the south, with a *gare routière* next to the main mosque.

There are buses for **Marrakech**, **Casablanca** and **Beni Mellal**. *Grands taxis* in Landrovers (2 a day) and Mercedes transit vans (2 a day) to **Tabant**; Landrovers for **Zaouïat Ahansal**, too, although for this destination it is probably best to get a Peugeot or Mercedes *grand taxi* to Ouaouizaght and then switch to the less comfortable Landrover.

Beni Mellal *p101*

CTM buses leave from the terminal in the town centre. Connections with **Marrakech** and 3 a day for **Fès**. From the bus station it is a 10-min walk up Av des FAR to the centre. **Casablanca** service irregular.

Grands taxis up to **Ouaouizaght** and to **Azilal**, whence you can pick up tougher transport to the **Aït Bougmez** and **Zaouïat Ahansal**.

Kasbah Tadla *p101*

CTM buses for **Fès**, **Marrakech** and **Beni Mellal** run via Kasbah Tadla. Private line buses from **Agence SLAC** for **Beni Mellal**, **Boujaâd** and **Oued Zem** and **Rabat**. These can all be caught from the bus station on the Boujaâd side of town (ie the far side to the old kasbah).

Boujaâd *p101*

Regular buses and *grands taxis* leave for **Kasbah Tadla** and **Oued Zem** from the main square.

Imilchil *p102*

A long way from anywhere else, Imilchil is hard to reach unless you have your own transport, though you might find a *grand taxi* going that way from the north on the market days of Fri and Sun.